The Medieval World

LANDMARKS OF THE WORLD'S ART

THE MEDIEVAL WORLD

PETER KIDSON

Conway Librarian, Courtauld Institute of Art, London

PAUL HAMLYN · LONDON

General Editors

TREWIN COPPLESTONE   BERNARD S. MYERS
London   *New York*

PREHISTORIC AND PRIMITIVE MAN
Dr Donald Strong, Assistant Keeper, Department of
nology, Munich

THE ANCIENT WORLD
Professor Giovanni Garbini, Institute of Near Eastern
Studies, University of Rome

THE CLASSICAL WORLD
Dr Donald Strong, Assistant Keeper, Department of
Greek and Roman Antiquities, British Museum, London

THE EARLY CHRISTIAN AND BYZANTINE WORLD
Professor Jean Lassus, Institute of Art and Archaeology,
University of Paris

THE WORLD OF ISLAM
Dr Ernst J. Grube, Curator, Islamic Department,
Metropolitan Museum of Art, New York

THE ORIENTAL WORLD
Jeannine Auboyer, Keeper at the Musée Guimet, Paris
Dr Roger Goepper, Director of the Museum of Far Eastern
Art, Cologne

THE MEDIEVAL WORLD
Peter Kidson, Conway Librarian, Courtauld Institute of
Art, London

MAN AND THE RENAISSANCE
Andrew Martindale, Senior Lecturer in the School of
Fine Arts, University of East Anglia

THE AGE OF BAROQUE
Michael Kitson, Lecturer in the History of Art, Courtauld
Institute of Art, London

THE MODERN WORLD
Norbert Lynton, Head of the School of Art History and
General Studies, Chelsea School of Art, London

PUBLISHED BY
PAUL HAMLYN LIMITED · DRURY HOUSE
RUSSELL STREET · LONDON · W.C.2
© PAUL HAMLYN LIMITED 1967

PRINTED IN THE NETHERLANDS BY JOH. ENSCHEDÉ EN ZONEN
GRAFISCHE INRICHTING N.V.   HAARLEM

Previous pages: The Flight into Egypt. Capital from Autun
cathedral.

List of Contents

Colour Plates

Opposite: Gislebertus. 'The Weighing of Souls.' Detail from the Last Judgment tympanum, Autun cathedral.

Introduction

The numbers in the margins refer to the illustrations: heavy type for colour plates, italics for black and white illustrations.

Late in the 2nd century BC two German tribes known to Latin historians as the Cimbri and Teutones left their homelands in Jutland and began a long march southward, which by 113 BC had brought them to the confines of Italy. There, as much to their own surprise as to the consternation of their enemies, they contrived to defeat one Roman army after another, and for a period of some twelve years it seemed to the Italians as though the terrible invasions of Hannibal and the Gauls were about to be repeated. Eventually, the danger was averted by the military genius of Caius Marius, and a superficial observer might easily have concluded that a transitory episode was at an end. But in fact this first recorded encounter between Romans and Germans was fraught with immense consequences for the future. The totally unexpected renewal of danger from the north, after a century of unbroken victories in the coastlands of the Mediterranean, touched the pride, the complacency and fear of the Romans in a spot that was inordinately sensitive. Accordingly in due course they embarked on a policy of conquest in north-western Europe that was designed to put an end once and for all to any further threat to their security from that quarter.

With the partial implementation of this northern policy of Rome, which began with Caesar's invasion of Gaul in 58 BC and ended with the destruction of Varus' legions in the Teutoburg Forest in AD 9, a new situation was created. Within the Roman world a new balance was established between East and West, and a whole new set of relations were formed with peoples beyond the Roman frontiers. Although the occupation of Gaul was primarily a military affair, it had the effect of extending the frontiers of the classical world beyond the limits of the Mediterranean, to include the greater part of north-western Europe. The Latin language and pockets of Latin culture took root throughout the region. In Burgundy, the Rhône valley, on the Mosel and the left bank of the Rhine below Mainz, buildings were erected which, if modest by the standards of Rome itself, were sufficient even in ruin to evoke for later generations who saw them images of surpassing splendour. Not least, a system of roads was devised which presupposed that nearly everyone who travelled wished to travel to Italy; and this characteristic orientation survived the military and political links that gave it sense. The stamp of all this has proved indelible. In spite of the upheavals of the centuries that followed, north-western Europe was never quite able to forget that it had once been Roman.

Nevertheless, granted that there would have been no Europe as we understand it if the legions had not marched northward, it is necessary to make two very important reservations. The first is that in creating an Empire beyond the Alps, the Romans took the forms and features of Mediterranean life into regions whose climate, landscapes and peoples were utterly different from those of the Mediterranean itself. As the Greeks before them had found when they tried to transplant their own way of life abroad after the conquests of Alexander the Great, classicism apparent-

2

ly could not flourish too far from its native sea. The further north the frontier went, the more superficial, diluted and compromised were the authentic patterns of Roman life. North of the Loire, except on the frontiers themselves, traces of the occupation are slight compared with those in the south. No doubt much has been effaced in the northern provinces; but at least part of the explanation for the effacement lies in the fact that this was relatively easy to accomplish.

The consequences of these inequalities of emphasis in the inheritance that Europe received from classical antiquity were no less important than the inheritance itself, for the distribution of Barbarian settlements after the collapse of Roman government in western Europe had the effect of accentuating the differences. France in particular was deeply affected by the ambiguities inherent in this situation. All through the Middle Ages and beyond, her Janus-faced position at the centre of the cultural life of Europe stemmed ultimately from the fact that she had once belonged, yet never wholly belonged, to the Mediterranean world.

The second reservation is even more important. The Roman conquests were partial and incomplete. Presumably on the grounds that the danger did not justify the effort, an outer Celtic fringe was left unsubdued in Scotland and Ireland. In the event this turned out to be a miscalculation. By the 4th century the Picts from Scotland were proving a serious menace to the province of Britain. Moreover the Irish, after centuries of docile obscurity beyond the horizons of the Empire, responded to its dissolution by taking it upon themselves to preserve and transmit whatever garbled fragments of Christian and classical learning had come their way. This presumptuous intervention of the un-Romanised Irish in the cultural life of early medieval Europe proved an episode of considerable importance for the dissemination, if not the actual creation, of some of the weirder forms of Barbarian art.

1, 11, 12

But the really decisive failure of the Romans was against the Germans. If the conquest of Gaul was undertaken to provide Rome with inviolable frontiers, it is unlikely that the Rhine was chosen for this purpose in the first instance. Caesar's own punitive forays into Britain and Germany foreshadowed developments of Imperial policy. During the 1st century AD the campaigns of Claudius and Agricola brought the greater part of Britain under Roman control; and for some years at the turn of the era Augustus clearly entertained the far more important project of subduing the Germans. But the latter after their success against Varus managed to elude a similar fate. With surprising meekness the Romans seemed to have accepted the verdict of the Teutoburg Forest, and henceforth their frontier stopped short at the Rhine. So the Germans, unlike most of the Celts, remained free and outside the Empire.

2

It would be anachronistic to gild this victory with the lurid colours of 19th-century nationalism. At the time the Germans do not seem to have been unduly impressed by

1. **Cross at Ahenny, County Clare,** Ireland. 8th century. The elaborate carving of the high crosses that were popular in Ireland between the 8th and 12th centuries contrasts with the simplicity of the churches of the same period. This early example is covered with interlace comparable to that found in contemporary metalwork and manuscripts (figures 11, 12).

2. **The Aula Regia, Trier.** Early 4th century. The Imperial hall at Trier, in the Roman frontier region east of the Rhine, one of the most impressive reminders in northern Europe of the architectural achievements of the classical world, was a source of inspiration throughout the early Middle Ages. It was the model for Charlemagne's hall at Aachen (p. 41) and almost certainly inspired the giant wall arcades found in the Imperial cathedrals of the 11th and 12th centuries.

their success. It left no mark on their legends or folk memory. Many centuries were needed for the full implications of the Roman failure to become evident. The first thing to realise is that the defeat in no way put an end to dealings between Romans and Germans. It merely altered the terms on which these were destined to be conducted. Instead of having Roman civilisation imposed upon them from above in one sudden and overwhelming dose, as happened to the Gauls, the Germans slowed the whole process down to their own pace, and took what they wanted from their neighbours only when they were ready. We know almost nothing in detail about these early transactions. But if we compare what Tacitus wrote about the Germans in about 100 AD with Caesar's remarks 150 years before, it is clear that they had already learnt much, especially about agriculture, commerce and war. Three hundred years later, when at last they emerged into the light of history, many of them no longer deserved to be called 'Barbarians' —at least in the pejorative sense of the word.

In material and technological respects, they were probably not far behind the Romans. By assimilating the elementary forms of civilised life in this piecemeal way, the Germans did not cease to be German. Above all, their independence allowed them to remain formidable—unlike the Gauls who, once they had become Roman provincials, more or less ceased to take an active part in shaping the events of history. In fact, the Germans became more and more formidable, so that from the middle of the 3rd century AD it was no longer a question of Romans conquering the Germans, but of Germans conquering the Romans.

This is no place to recount the long and complicated story of how the various German kingdoms were established among the ruins of the western provinces of the Roman Empire. For us what matters is that these events brought the Germans, or at least some of them, face to face with the more sophisticated aspects of Roman life, such as religion, law, literature, architecture and the figurative arts. Until this happened their initiation into the higher mysteries of civilisation could hardly proceed. But here we encounter one of those great paradoxes, about which historians have never ceased to wrangle: for it would seem that in order to become civilised themselves in this more profound sense the Germans had to destroy the only civilisation from which they could learn.

THE IDEA OF A 'MIDDLE AGE'

The extent to which the German invasions were responsible for the fall of the Roman Empire has been assessed in many different ways ever since the Renaissance. It is perhaps no accident that the first people to blame them outright for the catastrophe were the earliest Italian humanists, archaeologists and art historians, whose picture of events is neatly summarised in the terminology which they invented and which we still use for the epochs of history, i.e. ancient, medieval and modern. The idea of a 'Middle Age' could only occur to men for whom the past was, so to speak, split in two. On the one hand there was a past that was both precious and remote—something that was infinitely worth recovering, but which could be recovered or recreated now only because it had ceased to be long ago.

3. **Proserpina sarcophagus.** 2nd–3rd centuries. St Michael's chapel, Aachen minster. This sarcophagus, according to tradition, was reused for the tomb of Charlemagne, and with its elaborate composition of animated figures is an example of the type of classical sculpture that must have been known throughout the Middle Ages, although it was only at times a direct source of inspiration to medieval sculptors.

4 (opposite). **Front panel of a reliquary.** 8th–9th centuries. Oak. Abbey church, Werden. The crude representation of Christ on this reliquary, possibly of Irish or Anglo-Saxon origin, illustrates the lack of interest in a naturalistic figure style that was a legacy of the pre-Christian artistic traditions of northern Europe.

On the other hand there was a more recent past, stretching like a gulf of time between the present and the past that really mattered. So far as literature and the arts were concerned this was precisely how many learned and influential Italians felt, from Petrarch in the 14th century to Flavio Biondo in the 15th and Vasari in the 16th. Between them these and other men of like mind successfully launched the mutually complementary concepts of the decline and fall of classical antiquity and the Renaissance. The intervening Middle Age, devoid of all merit, was ushered in by the German invaders, among whom the Goths were singled out for special notoriety, by reason of their alleged part in the destruction of Rome itself. (Hence the term 'Gothic', which has remained part of the vocabulary of art history ever since, although its meaning has changed much since the days when it was a term of abuse, synonymous with both barbaric and medieval. The name of the Vandals, another German tribe, whose qualifications for the part were probably better than those of the Goths, still has this Renaissance connotation.)

It may be said at once that this attitude toward medieval history, as beginning with the overthrow of Rome and ending with the recovery of Roman civilisation, has long been recognised as inadequate, especially by historians (as apposed to art historians). But it does not follow that this is a point of view wholly devoid of insight or truth. So far as the arts are concerned, even if we manage to avoid the emotional attitudes and value judgements of the Renaissance, it is abundantly clear that for many centuries German societies in the west had little or no use for the achieve-

ments of classical antiquity and, whether through ignorance, neglect or wilful perversity, they did in fact destroy far more than they preserved. If the Renaissance picture of the Middle Ages is wrong, it is not because it does excessive violence to the evidence, but because it is essentially too simple. What these earliest historians failed to realise were the complications that arose partly from the different circumstances in which different groups of Germans found themselves when they began to adjust to their Roman environment, partly from the discordant elements embedded in the civilisation they inherited, and partly from the attitudes of the Germans toward their inheritance. When allowances have been made for these aspects of the matter, the Middle Ages are apt to appear in a somewhat different light.

If we stand far enough back and regard the thousand years of European history between 400 and 1400 as a whole, with antiquity at one end and the Renaissance world at the other, the negative aspect of German indifference toward Rome becomes less important than German attempts to come to terms with Rome and all that it implied. For Rome was synonymous with civilisation itself, and unless the Germans were to thwart their urge to civilise themselves, they had no option but to model themselves on the Romans, and indeed in a manner of speaking to become Romans. From this point of view, the Renaissance began when the Germans arrived on the scene, and took a thousand years to work itself out.

One reason why the process of assimilation took so long is that it was not political. At the outset, while Rome re-

mained great, the Germans had grown used to the status of exclusion—Romans were Romans and Germans were Germans. Strange as it may seem, this sense of separate identity was heightened rather than lessened by the German conquests. Whereas before they had wanted nothing better than to break into the Empire, afterwards they turned in on themselves and became conscious once more of the fact that they were racially and socially apart. To some extent no doubt this was due to the disdain of the conquerors for the conquered. But the crux of the matter was their total inability to comprehend the literary culture that confronted them. In a sense we may think of the culture of the ancient world as part of the plunder which fell to the Barbarians by right of conquest. But precisely because they took possession of it by force, they were never in the position of being directly taught by the Romans and consequently had no idea what to do with it. Apart from a few farsighted Romans such as Boethius and Cassiodorus in the 6th century, who saw that the future lay with the Barbarians and thought it was their duty to educate the new masters, there was no one to show them how. So in the event, there was no alternative but for them to teach themselves, and make what use of it they could. Being under no pressure to learn they did so in leisurely, perverse and fitful ways. They made endless mistakes and got things confused. In the manner of _4, 15_ children they often seemed to have been performing some ludicrous masquerade or elaborate caricature of their elders and betters. But if we think of them in this way we must also remember that the only elders and betters in the world for most of the time in question were far away in

Byzantium and the Muslim world, and that like children they took themselves absolutely seriously. Moreover it was a continuous process. We tend to speak of a Carolingian renaissance, or the renaissance of the 12th century as though they were isolated spurts of energy separated by intervals of stagnation. But although this habit has a certain value of convenience, it is apt to conceal a crucial feature of the matter, namely that there was seldom any considerable period of time during the Middle Ages when somebody's attention somewhere in Europe was not concentrated on some aspect or other of the inheritance from antiquity. Instead of arranging the phenomena of renaissance chronologically, it is perhaps more illuminating to classify them according to their content. In the first place it was religion. However providential we may be disposed to regard the conversion of the Barbarians, the fact remains that for them Christianity was the religion of the Romans. Indeed, apart from the army, it was the first department of Roman life which they were actually invited to share. By becoming Christian the Barbarians established a kind of fraternity with the Romans over against the rest of the world, and this in effect opened all other doors to them.

In the wake of religion came the political theory of the later Roman Empire. Charlemagne in the 8th century, the Ottonian and Salian rulers of Germany in the 10th and 11th centuries, Frederick Barbarossa in the 12th century, and Frederick II of Sicily in the 13th were all deeply concerned with the implications of the Imperial title, and during their respective reigns it often seemed as though medieval Europe was on the point of entering into the political **13** heritage of Rome. Much early medieval art is in fact Imperial propaganda. But whereas the consequences of the Barbarian conversion to Christianity were both endless and permanent, the medieval Empire was never wholeheartedly accepted as the right and proper framework for the development of European society. Responsibility for these inhibitions rests ultimately with the Church, or more precisely with the Pope. For the medieval Papacy no less than the medieval Empire was grounded in Roman concepts of law and government, and in the event the antipathy of the Popes to the implications of Imperial power brought about the downfall of the Empire.

What it came to is that the Popes eventually saw themselves as the true successors of the Caesars, and the Church whether by design or accident found itself from the turn of the millennium onwards the guardian and promoter of classical learning. At the outset only a few remarkable individuals were involved. Men like Gerbert of Aurillac (Pope Sylvester II) and Fulbert of Chartres were inspired by much the same attitude toward antiquity as their more numerous successors in the 12th century; and if their renaissance was more superficial than that of their successors this was because they operated more or less singlehanded. It took time for the processes of scholarship to acquire momentum. The more difficult and delicate achievements of antiquity in the fields of philosophy, literature and natural science were only fully appreciated towards the end of the Middle Ages, and only slowly disentangled from the more familiar preoccupation of medieval people with religion. The same is true of the arts. As the rest of this book is devoted to them as a special case, there is no need at this point to anticipate what follows. All that concerns us here is the overall picture, and it is sufficient to indicate that the arts in no way depart from the general pattern of development. However improbable it may seem at first sight, nearly every important change that occurred in the history of medieval art took place under the catalytic auspices of some aspect of what had been handed down from the ancient world.

From this point of view it is tempting to regard the Italian Renaissance, the Renaissance proper, as nothing more than the last and most sophisticated stage of a process that had begun before the Roman Empire in western Europe had even disappeared. Up to a point this is true. Nevertheless, it would be a mistake to think of the Middle Ages as a period wholly given up to the systematic and painstaking exploration of what survived from antiquity. In the first place no one thought of it as an inheritance, and no one thought of the ancient world as we do. There were simply books and buildings, ideas and precedents, for which uses could be found when the occasion arose. This idea that the symptoms of antiquity which we encounter throughout medieval history were connected with practical problems and contemporary situations, that antiquity was so to speak used rather than revived, is vital. Thus it was the military and political clarification which followed the conquests of

Charlemagne that invited the generation of AD 800 to regard him as a veritable Roman Emperor—not the other way round. Again, in the 12th century when Europe was avid for knowledge, any source of learning would do. In a sense there was ultimately no alternative to antiquity, but what came via the Arabs was just as eagerly accepted. Perhaps not until Aristotle obtruded on the attention of 13th-century theologians did a really critical test case arise. By then it was possible for the words of an ancient writer to strike a note that was both too important to be ignored and at the same time recognisably discordant. It is highly illuminating to observe the effects of this shocking realisation on sensitive medieval minds like that of St Thomas Aquinas, and the incredible efforts that were made to reconcile the ostensibly irreconcilable factors in the case, and coopt Aristotle into what was essentially a contemporary debate.

In this long and complex encounter between the Middle Ages and antiquity, the latter was essentially passive and pliable. Not until the Italian Renaissance, when the concept of classical antiquity was clearly formulated for the

first time, was the past completely disentangled from the present and in a position actively to impose its own forms and attitudes on living men. This is the crucial sense in which the Italian Renaissance can be distinguished from the Middle Ages. It is not so much a question of the Italians being more closely concerned with antiquity than with the Middle Ages, but of them thinking about the past in a different way. The Italian humanists made an ideal out of antiquity. It provided them with a new yardstick of excellence whereby they could judge men, literature and art. But this vision could be apprehended only by the exercise of new intellectual skills. In effect it was a kind of archaeological reconstruction—if somewhat too rosy by modern scientific standards. Together with their new consciousness of temporal distance, it introduced them to something recognisable as history. There was nothing corresponding to this in the Middle Ages. Not only was medieval chronology both rudimentary and vague, but in so far as it can be said to have existed at all everything was related to a single event—the Incarnation. Taken literally, as of course it

was, this intrusion of an eternal God into a transitory world had the effect of enveloping time in timelessness; and instead of the historical sense of everything receding away from the present into an ever more remote past, there were so to speak two absolute moments set over and against one another in an abrupt and static antithesis—before and after, then and now, BC and AD.

PAGAN AND CHRISTIAN

The consequences of this medieval way of thinking about time were almost endless. For our purposes, however, we may single out its obvious relevance to the distinction between pagan and Christian. Not every pagan lived before Christ, but everyone who had done so was *a fortiori* pagan, and this of course included all classical antiquity.

Medieval attitudes toward the pre-Christian past varied so much that it is reckless to generalise. Nevertheless they seem to have gravitated in two opposite directions. On the one hand there was the feeling, already widespread in antiquity itself, that pagan culture was a snare and delusion

5 (opposite). **Ascension of Christ.** 4th–5th centuries. Ivory. Bayerisches Nationalmuseum, Munich. Easily portable Early Christian works such as this ivory were frequently copied in Carolingian times. The form of the Holy Sepulchre seen here derives from pagan Roman tombs (compare it with the towers of St Riquier, figure 20).

6 (right). **St Augustine.** Page from St Augustine's *De Civitate Dei* (MS. Plut. XII, 17, f. 3v). Early 12th century. 13¾ × 9¾ in. (35 × 25 cm.). Biblioteca Laurenziana, Florence. The ideas in St Augustine's *City of God* were of fundamental importance to medieval thought (see p. 14). This page showing St Augustine, which comes from a copy made at St Augustine's abbey, Canterbury, demonstrates how English illumination of the early 12th century combines Anglo-Saxon artistic traditions (figures 23, 24) with new continental elements (compare plates 47, 48).

13

7. **The Franks casket.** Late 7th century. Whalebone.
l. 9 in. (23 cm.). British Museum, London. This casket is
decorated with both pagan and Christian subjects—a
confused mixture typical of this period of English culture
(compare plate 1). Note how the details of this vigorous
narrative scene from Norse mythology cover the entire surface.

for the prudent Christian soul. As Tertullian put it in his
famous rhetorical question: 'What has Athens to do with
Jerusalem?' It was a position congenial to men of strong
will and austere temperament, and a point of view that
was always liable to receive expression from powerful puri-
tans such as St Bernard in the 12th century, or humble con-
templatives like St Thomas à Kempis in the 15th.

But it was equally possible to think of Christianity as the
consummation rather than the antithesis of classical culture. This was the approach of a number of learned and
cultivated writers of the early Christian period, such as
Clement of Alexandria and the Cappadocian Fathers. In
his *Civitas Dei (The City of God)* St Augustine presented the
presuppositions of this view of history so plausibly that it
was a thousand years before any real alternative was
worked out. From this standpoint the ancient philosophers
and even poets like Virgil could be regarded in much the
same way as the Old Testament prophets; and the study of
ancient letters could be justified or excused on the grounds
that it was conducive to 'the better understanding of the
mysteries of the divine scriptures', to use a formula which
Alcuin wrote into one of Charlemagne's capitularies.
Being in possession of the true faith, medieval Christians
consulted the classics, if not actually in a spirit of condes-
cension, at least with a consoling smugness that came of
knowing higher truths than any accessible to pagan authors.
On the other hand, especially after the tidying up of
Church doctrine and the extension of papal control down
to the lower echelons of the ecclesiastical hierarchy which
followed the great reform of the 11th century, the Church
tended to become increasingly sensitive to the dangers of
heresy, and there was seldom a shortage of zealous churchmen who were prepared to recognise, not always tacitly,
that a line had to be drawn somewhere. Pagan literature
was never formally proscribed, but after the suppression

of the Albigensians in the south of France during the first
half of the 13th century ecclesiastical indulgence was tempered by a good deal of moral circumspection. There was
always a danger that if people read the classics they would
read Ovid; and for those who were prepared to penetrate
its more seductive and less edifying aspects, like Tann-
häuser, antiquity could be regarded as a temptation either
to be risked or resisted.

It is very important for us to realise that this fundamental antithesis between what was pagan and what was Christian was itself part of the Barbarian inheritance from antiquity. It is relatively easy for us to disentangle what was
distinctly classical in origin from what came to the Middle
Ages chiefly through the agency of Christianity from the
East. But the German Barbarians were not in this same for-
tunate position, and in fact it was only in terms of the distinction between pagan and Christian that they were able
to apprehend the classical past until quite late in the
Middle Ages. They were not to know that the culture of the
world upon which they burst, the later Roman Empire, was
itself undergoing fundamental changes at the very moment
of their arrival on the scene. The Romanisation of the
Barbarians was accompanied by another, quite distinct
but contemporary process, the Orientalisation of Rome.

This provides us with a quite different position from
which to contemplate the fall of the Roman Empire. If we
think of the Empire primarily as a political and military
institution, then its collapse in the West must inevitably to
some extent have been due to the external pressures of the
Barbarian invasion. But if we think of Rome as the last
guardian of the classical tradition which had been fashioned in Greece during the 6th and 5th centuries BC, then
the breakdown began long before the appearance of the
Barbarians. No doubt it is tempting to connect the breakdown of civilisation with the onslaughts of enemies whose

condition was admittedly barbarous. This is precisely what the historians of the Renaissance did. But the contribution of the Germans to the destruction of classical civilisation, though real enough up to a point, was both belated and superficial. The real spiritual crisis in which the traditional values of the classical world were put on trial and in great measure rejected occurred during the 2nd and 3rd centuries AD. From this point of view Gibbon's celebrated contention that Christianity had much to do with the fall of the Empire is valid. But it is not enough merely to lament the passing of the classical world. The plain fact of the matter is that by 200 AD classical culture had become little more than a literary affectation. The last resuscitation, which took place in the time of the Emperor Hadrian (see *The Classical World*), was itself oddly reminiscent of the Italian Renaissance. In so far as Christianity was responsible for exposing the bankruptcy of classicism, it also provided a genuine alternative, the superior attractions of which for the vast majority of men it is impossible to deny, and to whose more profound insights into the needs and status of human individuals classical learning had no answer.

The impeachment of the classical way of life which was conducted by pagan and Christian Emperors alike as well as the Doctors of the Church was extended to include classical art. For much the same reasons the classical tradition in art gradually lost any significance it might once have had for ordinary men, and it ended up as the rhetorical instrument of official propaganda. Even this function was taken away from it after 300 AD and from then on classical forms appear in art either as selfconscious revivals or disguised under heavy stylisation. In their place more often than not are to be found forms and styles whose purpose, *7* affiliations and bias were deliberately anti-classical.

There is no doubt that the Church was largely responsible for this revolution in taste. After the conversion the Church was in a position to have the art it wanted; and the truth is that it had little use for the classical kind. No doubt Pheidias, Polykleitos and the rest had perfected the classical style in the 5th and 4th centuries BC with the purpose of making the divinity of the gods visible to human eyes. But it required some very special metaphysical assumptions to imagine the gods in the ideal likeness of men, and the style easily degenerated into a vapid humanism. For most people, not trained in the discipline of Greek philosophy, it was easier and more satisfactory to think of the gods as *8* being different from men rather than like them, and they instinctively accepted the corollary that contact with a god transfigured or even deformed those who underwent the experience. These were the fundamental assumptions behind the transcendental stylised art of the ancient East, and for many Christians they were equally valid for any art destined to serve the needs of the Church. What the Church wanted was not perhaps the crude daubs of the catacombs, but the kind of art we encounter in the Early Christian *6,31,37* mosaics of Ravenna and Rome (see *The Early Christian and Byzantine World*). It is worth remembering, however, that

8. **Christ in Majesty.** Late 11th century. Marble. St Sernin, Toulouse. While the apostles in this series of reliefs at St Sernin (plate 36) reflect the influence of late antique sculpture, this stylised figure of Christ, with its highly finished marble surface, appears closer in style to low relief works on a smaller scale in ivory or metal.

9. **Wooden door of the stave church at Urnes.**
Mid-11th century. The woodcarving at Ornes has
given its name to the style of Scandinavian sculpture
characterised by this particular type of decorative
animal carving—a motif which, however, goes back to the
traditions of pagan secular art (compare figures 11, 12).
The lack of building stone in Scandinavia accounts for
elaborately decorated wooden churches such as this one.

the range of Early Christian art was as wide as the intellectual attitudes of the time. At one extreme there were
styles of which Tertullian might have approved—so saturated with other-worldliness as to involve a total repudiation of the classical tradition. At the other we find a measure of synthesis between classical naturalism and formal
abstractions which not unfairly reflects the outlook of cultivated Christians like Clement of Alexandria. This eventually matured into the stylised classicism of Byzantine art.

This was the state of affairs when the Barbarians appeared on the scene. In a sense the Middle Ages traversed
in art much the same range of experience as the ancient
Greeks. Like them they started from an almost exclusive
concern for abstract ornament, and ended up with the _1, 1, 11, 1_
kind of naturalism that springs from man's preoccupation _71, 73, 62_
with man. But unlike the Greeks they did not have to _63_
break new ground. At every turn they were liable to find a
suitable precedent, and their progress therefore takes the
form of penetrating back through varying degrees of stylisation to a position from which they could appreciate
classical naturalism for its own sake. Thus medieval art is _63, 64, 65_
apt to seem almost unduly obsessed with what already
existed. At the crudest level this took the form of mere copying. But even imitation required a measure of insight and
understanding, and in certain circumstances it also required the selection of some models and the rejection of
others. Hence the interest of medieval art historians in
identifying sources. All the really important changes, however, arose from the recognition of new needs, which in
turn required the consultation of new precedents. For it
was not the medieval way to invent where there was an
example to follow. Apart from Viking and Muslim ornament these precedents were nearly always found in the inheritance from antiquity. And so it came about that uses
were gradually found for more and more aspects of ancient
art. Whenever this happened on a large scale we encounter
the symptoms of a renaissance. But in every case these situations arose from contemporary problems, not from a special
desire to recreate antiquity for its own sake. That is why
none of the so-called medieval renaissances endured for _16, 70_
long, and why they made hardly any impression on the
fundamental presuppositions of society.

In a book of this size it is impossible to deal equally with
all the problems presented by such a vast period. No doubt
there is a certain injustice in focusing attention on the
period after the turn of the millennium rather than before.
On the other hand to reverse the stress would be even more
unjust. It should not be necessary to add that this somewhat old-fashioned distribution of emphasis does not entail
the view that medieval art was nothing more than a preparation for the Italian Renaissance, or that it can be
regarded as having a life cycle of its own. It is simply a
question of a series of historical changes from which the
overtones of biology that cling to our habitual terminology
must be rigorously excluded.

(Continued on page 33)

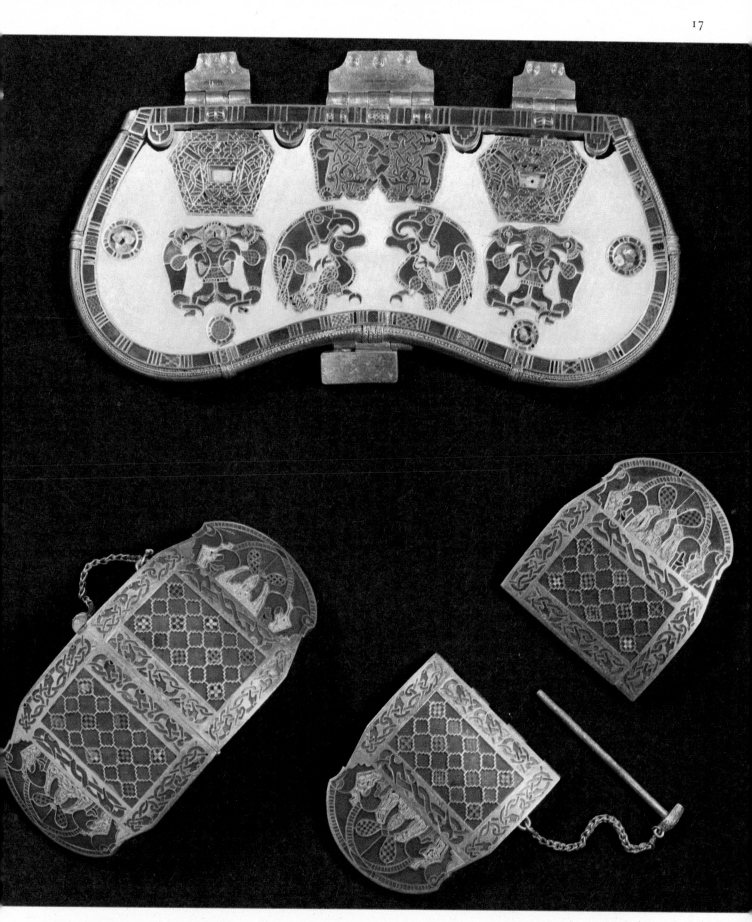

1. **Purse lid and clasps from Sutton Hoo,** Suffolk. Before *c.* 655. Gold, garnets and mosaic glass. Purse lid 7½ × 3 in. (19 × 8 cm.). British Museum, London. The Sutton Hoo ship burial, containing a rich collection of pagan grave goods together with objects probably of Christian significance, stands at the borderline between pagan and Christian. The skilled workmanship and elaborate designs found in these small portable personal adornments soon came to be applied to objects for the Church. Compare the interlaced animals on the clasps with the carpet page from the St Chad Gospels (figure 12).

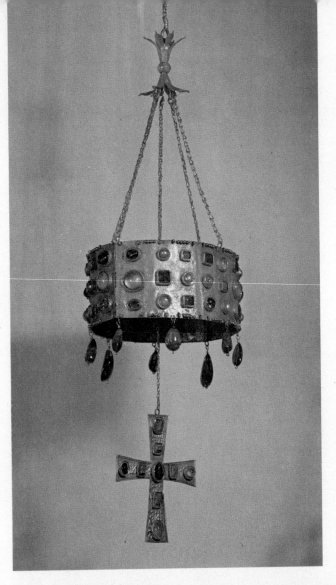

2. **Visigothic votive crown.** 7th century. Gold with precious stones. Cluny Museum, Paris. In 1858 a collection of eight votive crowns was discovered at Guarrazar, near Toledo in Spain. They are now divided between the National Museum, Madrid, and the Cluny Museum, Paris. From the name of Recceswinth, a 7th-century Visigothic king, that appears on all of them, and from the similarity of style, they can be dated to the last century of Visigothic rule in Spain.

3. **Frankish jugs.** 4th–6th centuries. Glass. Landesmuseum, Bonn. The Roman glass industry on the Rhine was one of several organised for industrial production to serve the needs of the army. When the Franks occupied the territories on the west bank these did not disappear at once, indicating that the change was not cataclysmic nor wholly destructive.

4. **Processional cross.** 7th century with 4th-century portrait medallion. Silver with gems and inset miniatures, etc. h. *c.* $43\frac{1}{4}$ in. (110 cm.). Museo Civico, Brescia. Often known as the Desiderius Cross. The embellishment of spectacular objects like this was often arbitrary, depending on what was available when it was made, and what was added later. The portrait may be of Galla Placidia with her children.

5. **Theodelinda's crown.** Early 7th century. Gold and precious stones. Cathedral Treasury, Monza. Theodelinda, the Christian wife of two successive Lombard rulers, took an active part in establishing peace between the Pope, the Eastern Empire and the new secular powers in northern Italy. This votive crown, which remains with other of her treasures at Monza, displays expensive materials rather than elaborate craftmanship. (Compare plates 1 and 2.)

6. **St Lawrence, Bradford on Avon.**
8th century or late 10th century. The
church is constructed of ashlar of quite
exceptional quality which may be reused
Roman masonry. William of Malmesbury
mentions a church at Bradford built by
St Aldhelm (8th century), which was still
there in his time (*c.* 1125). St Lawrence
has been identified as Aldhelm's church
on this testimony; but most of the detail is
usually regarded as belonging to the
period *c.* 1000. This kind of confusion is
typical of Anglo-Saxon architecture.

7 (opposite). **The scribe Ezra rewriting
the sacred records.** Early 8th century.
13¾ × 9¾ in. (35 × 25 cm.). From the
Codex Amiatinus (f. 5r). Biblioteca
Laurenziana, Florence. This
Northumbrian copy of an early Christian
manuscript succeeds to some extent in
reproducing the three-dimensional sense
of space found in the original, although
perspective, human form, light and shade
are copied without any real
understanding. Note the positions of the
left leg and foot, and the conflicting
perspectives of the cupboard.

8. **Exterior of the church of S. Miguel de Liño, Oviedo,** from the south-west. 9th century. After the Muslim invasion in the 8th century, the only part of Spain under Christian rule was the isolated kingdom of the Asturias on the north coast. S. Miguel de Liño, of which only the narthex and west part of the nave now survive, was one of the churches founded by Ramiro I (842–50).

9 (opposite). **St Matthew.** Before 823. From the Gospel book of Ebbo. 6¾ × 5½ in. (17 × 14 cm.). Bibliothèque Municipale, Epernay. Written at Hautvillers abbey for Ebbo, Archbishop of Reims, probably before his conversion of the Danes in 823 (as there is no reference to it in the dedication), this Gospel book is illustrated in a style which, although clearly dependent on late classical impressionism, also shows the Carolingian artist's interest in conveying spiritual intensity through dynamic calligraphy. Compare the Utrecht Psalter (figure 22).

10. **Back of altar antependium.** 835.
Gold and silver gilt, precious stones,
enamel and filigree. S. Ambrogio, Milan.
Master Volvinius, the artist of this
remarkable work (dated by the inscription
to 835), is shown with the donor, Bishop
Angilbert II, in the central roundels,
flanked by twelve scenes from the life of
St Ambrose. The arrangement of this
Carolingian altar, consisting of separate
panels with naturalistic figure scenes,
should be contrasted with the hieratic
architectural composition of the later
Basle altar (plate 22).

11. **The Master of St Giles.** *The Mass of St Giles* (detail). Late 15th century. Oil on panel. 24¼ × 18 in. (62 × 46 cm.). National Gallery, London. The picture shows St Giles celebrating Mass at the high altar of St Denis, on which are displayed the altar frontal of Charles the Bald, and the Cross of St Eloi. The latter, made for the Bishop of Noyon who died in 663, must have been one of the masterpieces of Merovingian metalwork (compare the Desiderius Cross, plate 4). The altar frontal was made late in the 9th century, probably at St Denis itself.

12 (opposite). **Cover of the Gospels of Gauzelin of Toul.** Late 10th century. Gold and precious stones, pearls, enamels. 12¼ × 8¾ in. (31 × 22 cm.). Nancy cathedral. Often as much care was lavished on the covers of religious books as on the illuminations inside them. Gospel books, being displayed and read during the celebration of the Mass, received a treatment comparable to other liturgical objects (compare plates 11 and 18).

13. **Holy water bucket.** *c.* 1000. Ivory, gold and precious stones. h. 7 in. (18 cm.). Aachen cathedral. This unique holy water bucket decorated with figures of Pope, Emperor and various ecclesiastics, with a row of guards underneath, may perhaps have been made for an Imperial coronation. It reflects the pomp and ritual of the Ottonian court, whose patronage was influential in all branches of art (compare plates 14 and 16). The jewelled bands are later additions.

14 (opposite). **Coronation of the Emperor.** 1002–1114. From the Bamberg Sacramentary (Cod. Lat. 4456, f. 11r). 11½ × 9½ in. (29 × 24 cm.). Staatsbibliothek, Munich. This illustration in the sacramentary given by Henry II to Bamberg cathedral shows the symbolic coronation of the Emperor, stressing his quasi-priestly function as *Servus Dei*. While the modelling of the faces reflects some contact with Byzantine art (compare plate 16), the stiff symmetrically arranged figures placed against flat ornamental frames and panels reminiscent of metalwork (compare plates 14 and 44) foreshadow many aspects of Romanesque art (compare plates 48 and 49).

15 (above). **Detail of crucifix** probably carved for Archbishop
Gero (969–976). Wood with traces of pigmentation. h. 74 in.
(188 cm.). Cologne cathedral. Once dated to the 12th century,
but now generally accepted as Ottonian. Large-scale figures in
wood and metal (compare plate 22) lead the way to
Romanesque stone sculpture (see figures 46, 94).
16 (below left). **Master of the Registrum Gregorii.** *Otto II
receiving the homage of the nations.* c. 983. From the Registrum
Gregorii. 10½ × 8 in. (27 × 20 cm.). Musée Condé, Chantilly.
This artist displays in his sense of pictorial space and the delicate

modelling of his figures a perceptive understanding of Early
Christian prototypes that marks a new departure in
Ottonian art.
17 (below right). **Christ the Saviour in the Tree of Life.**
Page from Gospel book (Cod. Lat. 4454, f. 20v). Early 11th
century. 12¼ × 9 in. (31 × 23 cm.). Staatsbibliothek, Munich.
This book, compared with plates 14 and 16 and with figure 25,
demonstrates the diversity of style which flourished under the
patronage of the Ottonian Emperors. Through their contacts
with Italy and the East, new artistic influences reached northern
Europe.

18. **The Lothar Cross.** 10th century. Wood covered with gold, filigree, precious stones, pearls, enamel. h. 19¾ in. (50 cm.). Aachen cathedral. Included in the carefully arranged composition of precious stones is a rock crystal seal of Lothar II from which the cross derives its name. Both the reused cameo of Augustus (perhaps meant to represent Christ) and the moulded capital-like terminals give this work a classical feeling comparable to that found in some Ottonian painting (see plate 16).

Pre-Romanesque Art

10. **King Theodoric pursuing a Stag into Hell.** 12th century. Stone. West portal, S. Zeno, Verona. In the *Nibelungenlied* the historical king of the Ostrogoths, Theodoric, was remembered as the legendary Dietrich von Bern. This is a very rare and early example of a secular theme from the German heroic age making its appearance in the predominantly religious art of the Romanesque period.

It is almost impossible to say anything about the art of the Barbarians before they encountered the Romans. Nothing whatever has survived from the first millennium BC, and by the time of the migration period (300–600) contacts were already numerous and well established. From the time of Septimius Severus onwards (*c.* 200) the industries which supplied the needs of the Roman armies on the frontiers became progressively more indifferent to the classical tradition; and as the number of German recruits increased it is almost possible to postulate an 'army style' to bridge the transition from late classical to Barbarian art. In any case Imperial diplomacy was largely conducted in terms of bribes and gifts, the forms of which were no doubt shrewdly adjusted to Barbarian taste. The earliest objects of Barbarian art come from hoards and graves extending from East Prussia to Rumania and the Crimea, and they betray a highly developed sense of pattern combined with an almost total indifference to the figure arts. Most of them were personal effects. Warriors were buried with swords, helmets and shields, women with brooches and trinkets. These were the prestige symbols of a primitive society, and their splendour was measured partly by the art, i.e. the

cunning, that went into their making, and partly by the intrinsic brilliance of the materials from which they were fashioned. This love of ornament was the one positive asset which they brought with them to their great encounter with the accumulated inheritance of Mediterranean art, and virtuosity in the working of metals or the construction of patterns out of jewellery outlasted the paganism with which it was originally associated. The treasures of the ship burial at Sutton Hoo (*c.* 655) which coincide with the end of pagan burial customs in East Anglia reveal the incredible sophistication of long-practised techniques which Christianity deflected rather than destroyed.

The character of Barbarian art after the migration period was largely determined by the numbers of the Barbarians themselves and the places in which they settled. The Goths who occupied Italy and Spain were not particularly numerous and they found themselves in the most intensely Romanised parts of western Europe. Their reaction is not unfairly reflected in the frank and famous remarks of one of their leaders, Athoulf, after his marriage to a Roman princess, Galla Placidia, in 414: 'At first I wanted to eradicate the very name of Rome, turn all the Roman lands into an Empire of the Goths, and to be myself what Caesar Augustus was. But I have learnt by experience that the Goths are too unruly to submit themselves to the law, and without law there can be no state. I have therefore chosen a more prudent way to glory by devoting Gothic energies to the increase of the name of Rome and I hope to be remembered by posterity as one who restored Rome because it was impossible for me to destroy it.' By and large the Goths lived up to this declaration of policy, more successfully perhaps in Italy than in Spain. So did the Lombards. Together they inherited the Early Christian

19 (opposite). **Golden Madonna.** Late 10th century. Wood covered in gold, filigree, precious stones, enamel. h. 29 in. (74 cm.). Essen minster. This work, the earliest surviving cult image of the Virgin and Child conceived as free-standing sculpture, reveals a striking understanding of three-dimensional form (compare the awkward figure of Ste Foi, plate 20). These new developments in Ottonian sculpture (compare plates 15 and 22), and also in painting (plate 16), must reflect increased contact with classical and Byzantine art.

culture of the Mediterranean which they modified only by debasement. Perhaps their most conspicuous contributions to the art of their time was in the form of sumptuous votive crowns with which the 7th-century kings of Visigothic Spain and Lombardy sought to emulate the gorgeous ceremonial and the mystery of consecrated kingship implied by the theory of Imperial government.

At the other end of the scale were the Anglo-Saxons. These were real Barbarians who moved from one peripheral area outside the Roman world to another within it. They ought thereby to have ensured for themselves a future tinged with mediocrity, but from this they were rescued by the ecclesiastical policy of Pope Gregory the Great (590–604). Papal dissatisfaction with the Caesaro-papism (control of the Church by the state) of Imperial Constantinople culminated in the resolve to reunite western Europe, not politically but ecclesiastically around the concept of orthodox Catholic Christendom with the Pope at its head. For a variety of reasons Britain offered a suitable base, and whether or not events transpired as Gregory planned, the Anglo-Saxon mission eventually completed the conversion of the residual German heathens and was instrumental in regenerating the established Church on the mainland of northern Europe.

One might have expected that the Roman mission to Britain would have imported Early Christian art into that country. On the contrary, however, we find an extraordinary willingness on the part of the Church to let Christian art there 'go native'. Only to a very limited extent can this be explained as tolerance of Barbarian ineptitude. A large element of deliberate policy was involved, and the outcome was important for the whole future development of Christian art, for the mere fact that henceforth there was an alternative to the Early Christian art of the Mediterranean introduced an element of polarity which in turn gave rise to stylistic tensions and the possibilities of interaction.

ANGLO-SAXON ARCHITECTURE

The two principal spheres of activity in which the implications of this far-reaching concession on the part of the Church may still be studied were church building and illuminated manuscripts. Whether or not any basilican churches were constructed in England after the arrival of St Augustine's mission in 597, the surviving traces of Anglo-Saxon architecture make it clear that they must have been exceptional. We know that the first Canterbury cathedral was a patched up Roman building, and that at the end of the 7th century Wilfrid built imposing churches at Ripon and Hexham, which may have reflected current Roman fashions. But the vast majority of Anglo-Saxon churches were of a different type altogether. Stripped of their accretions, they consisted essentially of boxes of masonry. The size, arrangement and proportions of these boxes varied, and the uses to which they were put are by no means all certain. Escomb in County Durham may be used

12 (above). **Carpet page.** St Chad Gospels (p. 220). 8th century. 9¾ × 7¼ in. (25 × 18 cm.). Lichfield cathedral library. Like the Lindisfarne Gospels, this book includes pages of pure ornament doubtless inspired by the decorative traditions of pagan art of the migration period (compare plate 1, figure 7). Writhing beasts like these remained popular, particularly in Viking art, until the 12th century (see figure 9).

11 (opposite). **The Tara brooch.** 8th–9th centuries. Gilt bronze, silver, glass, filigree, amber, enamel. National Museum, Dublin. The so-called 'Tara' brooch, which was carried off in a Viking raid in the 9th century and discovered with Scandinavian objects near the mouth of the River Boyne, is the finest surviving example of the exquisite Irish brooches that date from this period. The intricate patterns that were applied to this type of secular object were also used in the decoration of religious objects (compare figures 1, 12).

to illustrate the simplest type of plan with only two boxes, one for the nave and one for the chancel, while Reculver in Kent (669) shows a more complicated form. While it would be necessary to know much more than we do to explain these churches satisfactorily, it is evident that, in spite of occasional allusions to Mediterranean architecture, they have no counterparts in the Mediterranean world, and they can never have carried the same meaning as Early Christian basilicas. The main difference is in the architectural setting of congregation and altar. Instead of a unified hall with no more than an apse at the east end to house the altar, the little northern churches often tended to stress the contrast by making nave and chancel in effect separate if contiguous buildings.

It is tempting to relate this arrangement to the legal position of the Church in the Barbarian societies of northern Europe. Among the Germans the idea of an abstract corporation owning property was unfamiliar, and when they endowed churches they did so in a form which made no clear provision for the outright transfer of ownership. It is unlikely that their generosity towards the Church would have been as reckless as it appears to have been if it had entailed giving up all rights over the property in question. In effect what happened is that founders entered into a kind of treaty with the saint to whom the church was dedicated. The actual church buildings and the appointment of priests remained very much under the control of the founder and, although the saint enjoyed indirectly the yield of the endowments, the only thing he could be said to own was the altar, in which his presence was represented by a relic. This was the reason for the growing importance of relics, and helps to explain the widespread use of portable altars before relics became plentiful. This state of affairs, which persisted until the reform movement of the 10th and 11th centuries, meant that the lay influence was liable to be considerable and at times excessive. It also meant from an ecclesiastical point of view that the focus of attention shrank to a particular part of the church, the part which housed the altar. In fact in the last resort the altar itself became the only real object of religious devotion. The symbolic overtones of Early Christian architecture were either jettisoned outright or else drastically watered down.

A sense of contrast between nave and chancel, east end and west end, clergy and laity, was something towards which the practice of the Church had been moving for a long time. But this was the first overt architectural expression of the antithesis and, once established, in one form or another the idea was to go on affecting church architecture right through the Middle Ages. Furthermore, when architectural symbolism became an important factor in church design again, i.e. in Carolingian and Romanesque times, it was from the altar and the need to stress its meaning that the necessary imagery was largely drawn. So, in spite of their modesty, Anglo-Saxon churches represent a momentous new beginning.

ANGLO-SAXON MANUSCRIPT ILLUMINATION

Anglo-Saxon illuminated manuscripts indicate a similar point of view. From the end of the 7th century to the end of the 10th this particular kind of painting was perhaps more important than at any other time. Not that sumptuous manuscripts were more admired in the Dark Ages or that they ceased to be made later. But in the perhaps fortuitous absence of competition from the other arts, manuscript illumination assumes for a while a position at the centre of Christian art. During this period northern painting was heir to two very different traditions: on the one hand the decorative arts of the pagan Barbarians, with which must be included a problematic contribution from the already Christian Celtic fringe; and on the other the Early Christian art of the Mediterranean. In a sense the history of European painting during these three centuries is concerned with the interaction of these opposed strands, and with the gradual subordination of the former to the latter. During the first phase, however, before the so-called Carolingian renaissance, the Barbarian elements were very much in the ascendant.

The events that touched off the great outburst of artistic energy in northern England at the end of the 7th century are largely connected with the end of the independent history of the Celtic Church, and its submission to Rome at the Synod of Whitby (664). Christianity had penetrated to Ireland from England and Gaul in the 5th century, and it survived there more or less cut off from the rest of Christian Europe after the conquest of Britain by the pagan Anglo-Saxons. Some Christian literature seems to have found its

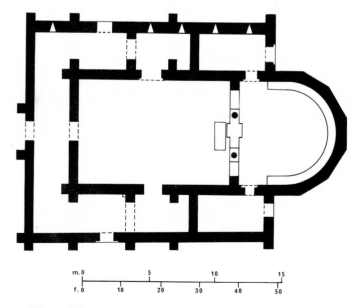

13. **Plan of Reculver,** Kent. 7th and 8th centuries. The church at Reculver was founded in 667. The original plan, as revealed in excavations, consisted of a chancel and nave separated by three arches resting on columns, with two flanking chambers to north and south. Later chambers were added further west.

way to Ireland, but if any Early Christian art did likewise, the traces were soon obliterated. The only links with the Mediterranean area that are observable in later Irish art seem to have been with Coptic Egypt. Such affinities are not so far-fetched as they might seem at first, because the form of Christianity which most deeply impressed the Irish was eremitic monasticism, whose original home was the Egyptian desert. But the early history of so-called Irish art is incredibly difficult to unravel. On the whole it is perhaps safer to think of the Dark Age Celts on either side of the Irish Sea as sharing a common way of life, the residue of a widespread culture which had been only superficially altered by the Roman conquest of north-western Europe. And it was probably the surviving Celtic societies on the western side of Britain, rather than the Irish themselves, who contributed most to the amalgam now generally called Hiberno-Saxon art.

Nevertheless the style itself seems to have been formed in Northumbria, and since the discovery of the Sutton Hoo treasure it has been acknowledged that the Anglo-Saxons contributed far more than the unduly publicised Celtic elements. Moreover it was only in Northumbria that books from the Mediterranean world were available to be copied. A special effort seems to have been made during the 7th century to supply Northumbria with outstanding Italian manuscripts. Some of these have in fact been traced to the Vivarium of Cassiodorus, a famous monastery in Calabria. One of the earliest copies made in Northumbria was the Codex Amiatinus now in the Laurentian Library at Florence. The famous Ezra miniature in this manuscript

must have been a passable rendering of its Early Christian original, and the fact that the book was immediately sent to Rome may account for the style of its illuminations. For home consumption, however, little or no attempt was made to reproduce either the colours or the spatial aspects of the model. This becomes obvious if the Codex Amiatinus is compared with the Lindisfarne Gospels (*c.* 700), the recognised masterpiece of the style. The Lindisfarne Gospels are one of those rare works of art, like the van Eycks' *Adoration of the Lamb*, for the perfection of which we are totally unprepared by its meagre precedents. It was a labour of love in honour of St Cuthbert, undertaken by his successor at Lindisfarne who wrote it, and by a goldsmith who covered the binding, now lost, with gold and gems. Each of the four Gospels was introduced by a portrait of the evangelist, a complete page of pure decoration and an incredibly elaborate initial for the first word of the text. The interest of the evangelists arises partly from their place in the gradual reduction of these images to the quality of playing-cards, partly from the destruction of their respective pictorial settings. There are still one or two suggestions of space around the Lindisfarne figures. A hundred years later, in the Book of Kells, everything had become two-dimensional outlines on the surface of the page. But it is the pages of abstract ornament and the initials that command our deepest respect. Celtic spirals, Roman key patterns and animal interlaces of Teutonic origin are disposed within their curious frames with a virtuosity that almost defies analysis. Apart from the rudimentary outlines of crosses, there are no traces of traditional Christian symbolism. The

14 (opposite). **Portable altar from Stavelot.** Mid-12th century. Silver gilt, champlevé enamel, bronze gilt. 4 × 6 × 9¾ in. (10 × 15 × 25 cm.). Musées Royaux d'Art et d'Histoire, Brussels. This fine example of a Mosan portable altar includes scenes of saints' martyrdoms in enamel, and bronze figures of evangelists at the corners. The increasing use made in the 12th century of virtually free-standing cast figures in metalwork (compare figures 53, 62) can be compared to the development of stone sculpture (see p. 78).

15. **St Luke.** St Chad Gospels (p. 218). 9th century. 9¾ × 7¼ in. (25 × 18 cm.). Lichfield cathedral library. Although the idea of an 'author portrait' derives from late classical manuscripts, this version of the evangelist shows how, to an even greater extent than in the Lindisfarne Gospels, the human figure has almost dissolved into abstract patterns under the influence of the traditions of non-representational art (compare figure 12).

patterns themselves have taken charge, and acquired a meaning that perhaps verged on magic.

It is both baffling and salutary to realise that this outlandish style was meant to serve the interests of religion, and that it flourished side by side with the active study of Christian and classical literature. The term 'renaissance' has been applied to these Northumbrian phenomena, but Hiberno-Saxon art brings out very forcibly just how selective the Barbarians could be in the uses they made of what the Mediterranean had to offer. At that stage even the relatively stylised forms of Early Christian art were beyond their grasp, and accordingly repudiated in favour of even more ruthless abstractions.

In a more restricted way Anglo-Saxon monumental sculpture deserves mention if only because it was practised at a time when scarcely anyone else in Europe had any use for this art form. A series of great stone crosses starting from the latter part of the 7th century show a typological development analogous to that of the manuscripts. When their decorative patterns, e.g. the vine scroll, are recognisably late antique, it is logical to presume that these come at the beginning of the series, and that when the vegetable forms are transmuted into abstract patterns they belong to its later stages. Whether such a tidy conceptual scheme provides a clue to chronology is another matter. But two of the earlier examples at Ruthwell and Bewcastle include figure sculpture which is remarkable for both its quality and its rarity. Later the Anglo-Saxons applied sculpture to the decoration of churches as well, and in this respect anticipated the tastes if not the methods of the Romanesque.

In a long-term estimate of the achievements of Anglo-Saxon art, there is much to be said for regarding them as did Vasari. If we think of European art during the first millennium as moving away from the norm of the classical ideal, this was as far as the process went (unless the Scandinavian animal styles are considered more outlandish). From the 8th century onwards there are symptoms of a movement in the opposite direction. Nevertheless it must be recognised that the 7th and 8th centuries were the crucial period in which the Barbarians acquired their fundamental grounding in the basic art forms of Mediterranean civilisation. In this sense their significant achievements have nothing to do with style at all. What mattered is that they built churches of stone or painted illuminated manuscripts or occasionally carved monumental reliefs. Otherwise the refinements of style had no context.

It was not the Anglo-Saxons but the Franks who took the decisive step of bringing northern art into permanent contact with the Mediterranean tradition. Of all the German tribes who crossed the Rhine in the 4th and 5th centuries the Franks were probably the most numerous and they did not move very far. They settled in a compact mass between the Rhine and the English Channel, including what had been the most highly developed part of the Roman Empire north of the Alps, i.e. the hinterland of the Rhine frontier. It was no accident that this area was to become the most highly industrial part of medieval Europe, and that the Roman skills of making glass, enamelling, and working metals were first relearnt here, if ever they had been entirely forgotten.

16. **Vine scroll.** Detail of frieze. 9th century. St Mary, Breedon on the Hill, Leicestershire. The Anglo-Saxon church at Breedon was originally decorated with sculptured friezes (now incorporated in a later building) which included this classically-inspired vine scroll motif, with birds pecking grapes.

The special contribution of the Franks to the development of Europe arose from historical circumstances that can only be briefly mentioned here. In a sense they prospered as the Byzantine Empire went into decline. On the death of the Emperor Justinian in 565 the Mediterranean seemed on the point of being reunited under the Imperial government of Constantinople, and it must have been a shock when the concealed weakness of the Empire was almost immediately exposed by the belated arrival in Italy of another tribe of Germans, the Lombards, who occupied large parts of that country. Nothing could be done to dislodge them, and henceforth, although the Exarch at Ravenna and the Pope at Rome in their respective capacities either embodied or acknowledged the formal claims of the Eastern Empire to rule Italy, in practice links between Italy and the East gradually assumed the status of fictions. In the 7th century the fortunes of the Byzantine Empire went from bad to worse. A ruinous bout of wars with Sassanid Persia was followed almost at once (*c.* 640) by the totally unexpected irruption of Mohammadan fanatics from Arabia. Neither Byzantium nor Persia were able to contain this avalanche. Persia succumbed altogether, while the Byzantine Empire in Asia shrank abruptly to the confines of Anatolia. Twice, in 681 and 717, it seemed as though the capital itself might fall to the Arabs. In the event this did not happen, but it was two hundred years before the Eastern Empire was in a position to carry the war back to this formidable enemy. Yet another line of attack threatened to take Europe in the rear. Along the south coast of the Mediterranean the Mohammadan tide proved irresistible. In 704 the Arabs took Gibraltar and in 732 they crossed the Pyrenees. Then at last at Poitiers in the heart of France they were stopped, decisively as it turned out, by the Franks under Charles Martel. If that verdict had gone the other way, it is conceivable that Christendom might have collapsed altogether. As it was, the two Christian successes, at Constantinople in 717 and at Poitiers in 732, ensured that Europe, both Eastern and Western, should survive, and they mark the point at which the fortunes of war began to even out.

Whether the internal life of Christian Europe was as deeply affected by the Muslim conquests as has sometimes been claimed, there is no doubt that they established the basic framework of medieval political geography. With the destruction of its age-long unity, the Mediterranean ceased to be a highway and became a frontier, Italy relapsed into a peripheral region and the centre of gravity shifted northwards. This was when Europe became Europe as we now know it. Moreover, instead of being drawn together by the gravity of their beleaguered situation, the components of Christendom tended to fall further and further apart. The European predominance of 6th-century Byzantium was never restored or replaced. In the West the vacuum was partially filled by the Frankish kingdom, the largest and most powerful of the Barbarian states. Around this polarity of power there imperceptibly developed a political antithesis between East and West which coincided with and underlined the ecclessiastical differences which had emerged in the century after Gregory the Great. This was the state of affairs in the middle of the 8th century when the Roman Church decided to break its residual connections with Constantinople and seek the more effective protection of Frankish arms in the face of imminent Lombard hostility.

By 750 everything conspired to select the ruler of the Franks as the only conceivable candidate for the vacant title of Emperor of the West. However, an ambiguous situation had developed which not only inhibited practical thinking in that direction, but also sheds curious light on the superstitions which surrounded kingship during the early Middle Ages. By the 7th century the patrimony of the ruling family, the Merovingians, had been dissipated to such an extent that the kings themselves were reduced to a state of political impotence. Effective power passed into the hands of aristocratic families near the throne who, like Japanese *shoguns*, disputed among themselves for control over puppet kings. By 687 the issue had been decided in favour of Pepin, the so-called Mayor of the Palace of Austrasia, i.e. the eastern and more German part of the Frankish kingdom. Pepin's descendants are known to history as the Carolingian dynasty. Their family estates were chiefly located in the vicinity of Liège and Aachen, the old Roman frontier region. It was not until 751 that papal sanction gave them an opportunity to retire the last of the Merovingians to a monastery (the only recognised method of deposition) and to assume the vacant crown. For only the Church controlled supernatural powers sufficient to abrogate the accumulated sentiment that surrounded one dynasty by shedding the aura of its approval on another. This was part of the price which Pepin exacted from the Pope in return for his armed intervention against the Lombards.

CHARLEMAGNE

What had been done once could be done again. In 800 Pepin's son Charlemagne (king 768–814) was formally crowned Emperor by the Pope in old St Peter's at Rome. For several hundred years afterwards ideas about Rome and the Roman Empire became a constant preoccupation with medieval publicists and artists. What they achieved, however, was saturated with all manner of ambiguities, and although in the final analysis the result was to attach Teutonic Europe more firmly than ever to its Mediterranean inheritance, the medieval Empire as such was largely self-deception. If many of the people concerned with its inception really took it seriously, this was due to Charlemagne himself. His personality must have been quite exceptionally overpowering. In an age when communications were bad and political cohesion depended almost entirely on the ability of a ruler to establish personal ascendancy over his vassals, Charlemagne appears to have had no difficulty at all in commanding obedience from Thuringia to the Pyrenees. He was a natural ruler, and when his biographer Einhard thought fit to borrow the Latin of Seutonius and flatter his subject by, so to speak, adding another to the *Lives of the Twelve Caesars*, more was involved than a literary conceit. As a conqueror, Charlemagne's reputation rests somewhat equivocally on push-over victories against the Lombards and Avars, and a very hard-won campaign against the Saxons, who were reluctantly though in the end effectively incorporated into the Frankish Empire by the expedient of enforced conversion (the alternative being massacre). To these may be added some posthumous and entirely fictitious successes against the Muslims in Spain which, however, in the literature of later ages gave him the lustre of an archetypal Crusader.

17. **Christ and Mary Magdalene.** Detail from a stone cross at Ruthwell. Late 7th century. h. 15 ft (457 cm.). The remarkable quality of the figure carving on this cross must reflect the close contacts with classical culture that existed in Northumbria at the time of the adoption of the practices of the Roman Church after the Synod of Whitby (compare figure 1).

18. **Aachen minster.** 9th century. Charlemagne built a palace and chapel at Aachen, one of his favourite residences. The chapel with its Italian-inspired circular plan and innovating and influential feature of a massive westwork still survives to the west of the Gothic choir.

19 (opposite, left). **The Symbolic Crowning of Otto II and Theophanu.** 982–3. Ivory. 7 × 4 in. (18 × 10 cm.). Cluny Museum, Paris. This ivory plaque showing Christ crowning the German Emperor Otto II and his Greek wife Theophanu is inspired by the kind of art produced by the Byzantine court. This is an important witness of artistic links with Byzantium, which help to explain the new developments in Ottonian art of this period (see plates 13–19).

20 (opposite, right). **St Riquier before 1090.** 17th-century engraving. This engraving after a drawing which is now lost, even if not entirely accurate, provides valuable evidence for the appearance of the exterior of this important Carolingian building where, as at Aachen (figure 18), particular attention was paid to the west as well as to the east end—a departure from the traditions of the Early Christian basilica.

Nevertheless he managed to bring together under one government all the continental Germans except the remnants of the Spanish Visigoths, and for a time there were only two powers in Christendom—the Greeks in the East and the Franks in the West. If the Franks thought of reviving the ancient Roman Empire in the West, this was partly because they were confronted by Imperial Byzantium. They looked sideways as well as backwards. The elevation of Charlemagne was one way of making plain that henceforth the West was on an equal footing with the East, and the Greeks had to concede that in spite of their inferior civilisation the Germans could no longer be excluded from a part in the political heritage of Rome.

But granted the great man, and the attitude of an age whose propaganda was habitually conducted in terms of symbols, the Carolingian Empire still seems like a literary charade mounted and stagemanaged by the scholars of the time. They alone had any idea of what Rome had been like in the days of its greatness, and they were the only people in a position to advise Charlemagne as to the form the renaissance should take. Not unfairly, perhaps, in the last resort the literary achievements were the ones that mattered most. Not a few ancient authors would have passed into oblivion but for the industry of Carolingian *scriptoria*. Whether Charlemagne himself really understood all that was done in his name and by his authority is another matter. No doubt he was content to bask in the reflected glory as a patron of art and letters. But it is difficult for us to see him now except through the eyes of his creatures, and therefore to disentangle the old Germanic warrior-hero with disgusting personal habits from the glowing image of scholarly wishful thinking.

The whole enterprise was inspired by the theory of the Christian Empire. But during the Middle Ages two very different interpretations of Imperial authority were current. One was that of the Byzantine Emperors, who saw themselves as God's viceroys on earth, a role which they chose to interpret as including the right to interfere in matters of Church doctrine. The other was that of the Roman Church, for which the Pope alone held God's commission to govern, and which was therefore inclined whenever possible to stress the indispensable contribution of the Pope to the making of an Emperor. It was not until the 11th century that the potential antagonism of these points of view came to the surface. During the Carolingian period the Church was not sufficiently organised as an international body to make an issue of its own claims, while the Carolingians themselves had too much need of the Church's cooperation to indulge in the hypothetical delights of Caesaro-papism. Nevertheless, precisely because each of these two positions was extreme, logically consistent and incompatible with the other, they define the limits within which all medieval Imperial art, not just Carolingian, was conceived. Any Western Emperor who took a high view of his office was liable to emulate the style of his Byzantine peers, and to recognise at Constantinople the kind of art that was most to his liking. Conversely those for whom the title was little more than an embellishment to the real substance of their power tended to make do with straightforward forms of Church art.

CAROLINGIAN ART

Charlemagne himself was probably the only Carolingian in a position to 'go Byzantine' if he had so wished. That he does not appear to have done so is largely due to the fortuitous circumstance that at the time the Byzantine world was still convulsed with controversy over iconoclasm. In the absence of contemporary inducements to copy the art forms of the Eastern Empire, and no doubt with papal approval, the Carolingians turned back to the past. In so far as they promoted a renaissance at all, it was fundamentally a renaissance of Early Christian art. In a sense they achieved what the Northumbrians had failed to do, namely to establish in northern Europe types of building and styles of painting whose ultimate place of origin was the Mediterranean. From this point of view Italy played a crucial role; and as the core of Carolingian power was in the north, artistic ideas and craftsmen began to flow from the south, from Italy to Aachen, fanning out from there to Tours and St Denis in France, and to the Rhineland and newly conquered Saxony in Germany. This traffic was to remain a fundamental feature of medieval art history until the development of the Gothic style.

But Carolingian art and architecture were more than just a renaissance. If the main impetus came from Italy, the 'minister of culture' himself, Alcuin, came from York, and with him the considerable strand of Saxon ornament that survives in Carolingian works. There was no conscious repudiation of Barbarian art, or official endorsement of Mediterranean styles. On the contrary we often get the impression that an effort was made to adapt the old forms to contemporary needs. This is perhaps most obvious in the palaces and churches. So much fuss has been made of the Roman features of Aachen and Ingelheim that it is as well to remember that they never lost the basic features of the traditional Teutonic *Hof*, the dwelling of a great man and his household. The basic formula was transformed, not replaced. The great hall at Aachen became a public building modelled on the Aula Regia at Trier, the most impressive Roman building north of the Alps. Likewise Carolingian churches were not so much Early Christian imports as the conflation of selected Early Christian forms with buildings whose function perhaps corresponded more closely to the Anglo-Saxon type. We know very little about northern Frankish churches before the Carolingian period; but it seems clear that few of them were simple Roman basilicas. The most important Carolingian contribution to the development of church architecture was perhaps a new conception of scale. From this time onwards we have evidence to sustain the distinction between great churches and small halls. Our knowledge of great Carolingian churches is fragmentary, and the best indications are provided by two drawings, one of the plan of an ideal monastery at St Gall in Switzerland (*c.* 820) and the other a drawing of the exterior of St Riquier (late 8th century). The St Gall plan provides our first evidence of the traditional Benedictine monastery of later times with the principal monastic buildings, including the church, set around a cloister. Although this general arrangement was reminiscent of a Mediterranean house-plan, the church itself had apses at both ends. This double-ended conception of a

great church was something of a Carolingian speciality, although it more often took the form of contrasting groups of towers or eastern and western transepts. Our earliest indication of what these churches looked like is provided by the St Riquier drawing in which a western block culminating in a staged tower was deliberately matched against a similar group at the crossing. Western blocks of this type had a long history in the following three centuries *86* before they finally turned into the two-tower façade of the Gothic cathedrals. Towers as such seem to have played little part in Early Christian architecture and, although the St Riquier towers remind us of Roman tower tombs and *5* representations of the Holy Sepulchre in Early Christian ivories, their incorporation into great church designs was a significant development of the new kind of medieval church iconography mentioned above.

The one really exceptional Carolingian building was the *18* palace chapel at Aachen. The connection of this with S. Vitale at Ravenna is well known, and nothing betrays the Imperial aspirations of Charlemagne better than this attempt to emulate his illustrious Imperial predecessors, from Constantine to Justinian, who had built centrally planned churches as part of or in close proximity to their palaces. Nothing like the Aachen chapel had existed in the north before and its influence was as widespread as that of the Sainte Chapelle centuries later.

When we turn to the decorative and figure arts, the Carolingian compromise between past and present becomes a straightforward confrontation of Early Christian and Barbarian art. The Barbarian contribution which came from both Anglo-Saxon and Lombard traditions, was chiefly felt in the field of ornament, while the impact of Early Christian forms was paramount in figure drawing. Our knowledge of Carolingian painting is entirely confined to illuminated manuscripts, although we know that the cupola of Aachen was covered with mosaics, and if the extant mosaics of Germigny des Prés are any clue it is likely that Byzantine craftsmen were employed. The range of style represented in surviving Carolingian manuscripts is surprisingly wide and suggests that any model would do providing it reached a sufficient standard of magnificence. So we find a fairly severe and not conspicuously classical figure style in the Godescalc Gospels at one extremity, and the ultra pictorial, impressionistic style of late antiquity represented by the Schatzkammer Gospels at Vienna on the other. The illuminations of the latter book were perhaps as close as Carolingian painting ever came to reviving a truly classical style, and it is interesting to observe the rapid transformation which this particular style underwent at the hands of its later practitioners. In the Ebbo Gospels *9* of the early 9th century calligraphy is already more important than paint, while in the Utrecht Psalter there is *22* nothing but outline drawing. It was in this last form that Carolingian art exerted its most far-reaching influence on

XXVII huic OAUID
OTEONECLAMA
BODSMEUSNESILEASA INLACUM MANUSMEASADTEM
ME NEQUANDOTACE EXAUDIDNEUOCEMDE PLUMSCMTUUM

21 (opposite). **Interior of St Cyriakus, Gernrode,** looking west. 10th, 11th and 12th centuries. The emphasis on the west end of a church (see figures 18, 20) often took the form in Germany of a western choir with its own apse, an alternative solution to a complex of chapels at the east end (figures 32, 33). Note the typically German features of alternating piers and columns, and the lack of vertical articulation (compare plate 21, figure 26).

22. **'Unto thee will I cry, O Lord.'** Detail of a page from the Utrecht Psalter (MS. 32, Psalm 28, f. 15v). $12\frac{3}{4} \times 9\frac{3}{4}$ in. (33×25 cm.). University Library, Utrecht.
23. **Crucifixion.** From Anglo-Saxon Psalter (B. M. Harley 2904, f. 3v). Late 10th century. Drawing $9\frac{1}{4} \times 7\frac{1}{4}$ in.

(23×18 cm.). British Museum, London. The Utrecht Psalter is illustrated with animated scenes which literally portray the words of each psalm, in a style that derives from the narrative illusionism of late classical painting. Its influence can be seen in the Crucifixion page from the 10th-century Anglo-Saxon manuscript, where however the agitated outline drawing is used not to convey movement, but to emphasise the emotions of the figures (compare plate 9, figure 24).

hic EST NAZARE
N IHC REX IUDEOR

the later Middle Ages, particularly on Anglo-Saxon 23 manuscripts. The Utrecht Psalter had found its way to England by the 10th century, and a whole tradition of outline drawing there was derived from it. Moreover this abstract drawing style can be detected in later Carolingian metalwork, such as the altar frontal which Charles the **11,14** Bald gave to St Denis.

It is important to realise the extent to which Early Christian styles were transformed to suit Carolingian tastes. From one point of view the process was not fundamentally different from that which we observe earlier in the British Isles. It may be unfair to attach undue importance to this trend, but it is necessary to bear in mind that technical progress in architecture and the greater interest in pictorial art which were the permanent achievements of the renaissance, were not in themselves sufficient to sustain the impetus of regeneration. During the 9th century there was a perceptible *rallentando* in which the high Imperial aspirations of the court of Aachen became progressively more isolated and deprived of their significance. Here we encounter the ultimate ambiguity of Carolingian art. Although it was a new beginning, it was too precarious and in a sense artificial to mature into a strong living tradition. And it is therefore perhaps nearer the mark to see it as the latest if also the most curious and hybrid of the sources from which medieval art drew its inspiration rather than as an integral part of medieval art itself.

Romanesque Art

In 910 and 911 three events took place which in a long-term view did much to shape the history of Europe during the next three hundred years. At Forchheim the leading dynasts of the eastern half of the Carolingian Empire met to elect a new king from among themselves. As a result, the bonds between Germany and the Carolingian dynasty were broken for ever, and Germany cautiously embarked upon the most brilliant period of her medieval history. During the hundred years that elapsed between the battle of the Lechfeld (955), when Otto I put an end once and for all to the Magyar menace in central Europe, and the premature death of Henry III in 1056, it must have seemed as though the future of Europe lay with the Germans, not with the French. In 962 Otto I was crowned Emperor at Rome, and the idea of the medieval Empire recovered some of the substance which it had lacked since the death of the Carolingian Lothar in 855. German art under the Ottonians and the Salians who followed them was inevitably coloured by these Imperial associations. In one respect it was a deliberate revival or even a continuation of 9th-century Carolingian art, although the emphasis differed somewhat in that Byzantine influence was now more overt. The reign of Basil II (976–1025) saw the high-water mark of the military fortunes of the Eastern Empire and the Germans consciously sought to associate themselves with its prestige through the marriage of Otto II with a Byzantine princess Theophanu (972) which was accompanied by the traditional exchange of works of art. But it would be a mistake to think of German art during this period as pursuing a course wholly different from that of the rest of western Europe. It was simply that Germany was the first part of Europe to emerge from the crisis of what has been aptly called the darkest part of the Dark Ages (c. 900) and, thanks to a strong central government and an enlightened clergy dedicated to the royal service, she got away to a flying start, both politically and in respect of artistic patronage. If this early promise was never quite fulfilled, it was largely due to entirely unforeseen circumstances after 1056. But in spite of the chronological accident that seems to separate Ottonian art from Romanesque, there is much to be said for seeing them as earlier and later phases of the same complex cultural phenomenon. And it is perhaps worth adding here that the other precocious artistic revival which took place in the 10th century, i.e. in Anglo-Saxon England, had a similar equivocal relationship with Romanesque art, being both a contributing source and an antithetical foil.

In France there was no counterpart to Forchheim until 987, when the throne passed to the Capetian dynasty. Nevertheless two events did occur in France in 910 and 911 which however inauspicious they may have seemed at the time were destined to mark an equally important turning point in the history of western Europe. The first was the establishment by Duke William of Aquitaine of a new kind of monastery at Cluny in French Burgundy not far from Macon. The other was an agreement, often dignified by

16

12,17

19

4,47, 25,
51

49, 24, 25

24. **Initial B.** Detail of a page from Anglo-Saxon Psalter (B. M. Harley 2904 f. 4r). Late 10th century. Initial 6¾ × 5½ in. (17 × 14 cm.). British Museum, London. Richly coloured frames and initials composed of forms inspired by classical acanthus foliage were popular features of late Anglo-Saxon illumination, which flourished side by side with figure drawing in the tradition of the Utrecht Psalter (see figures 22, 23). While the style of the latter gave way to new ideas in the 12th century, this kind of decorative initial was an important influence on the development of Romanesque ornament.

the name of treaty, made at St Clair sur Epte between Charles the Simple and the leader of a marauding band of Northmen whereby the latter were allowed to settle in the lower valley of the Seine. In their very different ways these two foundations, Cluny and Normandy, serve to illustrate two of the more important aspects of life in western Europe that determined the formation of Romanesque art. They are the reform movement in the Church and the remodelling of society on feudal lines.

26,28

It would be wrong to suppose that the depredations of the Northmen came abruptly to an end after 911 or that the Northmen themselves became docile. What happened was that their taste for violence was gradually deflected in a different direction—away from sheer plunder to the wider end of carving out for themselves large estates. At first sight this change hardly seems to constitute a constructive development. Feudal warfare in the 10th and 11th centuries must often have been cruel and savage, especially for the non-combatants. But although there was a great deal of wanton destruction the more enterprising protagonists always kept in mind the primary aims of creating enclaves of wealth and power. At a time when land was the only form of capital, and its yield the only sort of wealth that could be consumed or exchanged, the game of acquiring control over land was played with the same kind of ruthless zest that we find today in the commercial world of private enterprise, only with far fewer curbs and restrictions on their equivalents of our take-over bids. Every device was used—oaths of loyalty, guarantees of protection, marriages, blackmail, sheer blatant dispossession, and in the last resort killing. But out of the turmoil there eventually emerged throughout western Europe a landed aristocracy numbering at most ten thousand families, and with real power concentrated in the hands of a few hundred among them. By acquiring a stake in the land of France the Northmen qualified for cooption into this feudal aristocracy. They were to prove perhaps the most successful exponents of its techniques of aggrandisement; and by the 11th century they were outstanding among its members for their energy, intelligence and, not least, the range of their activities, which extended from Scotland to Sicily and the Balkans.

In the feudal world, no less than now, respectability was one of the rewards or penalties of success. In the 11th century respectability was equated with a certain kind of piety, which demonstrated itself by the endowment of religious foundations. These endowments seldom took the form of outright acts of alienation. For the most part they were regarded as investments whose value was twofold. On a purely mundane level, they functioned rather like trust funds, which left the benefactor an influence in the temporal affairs of the religious institution concerned, usually a monastery, often not far removed from total control. This was one way of making provision for the younger sons of the family, and it is not surprising to find during the 11th and 12th centuries that the upper echelons of the ecclesiastical hierarchy were recruited from the secular Establishment. The second advantage which these foundations represented brings us close to the heart of medieval religiosity. Granted that there were always individuals with insight into the spiritual character of Christianity, it remains true that for the vast majority of people, including the lay aristocracy, the operations of the Faith could only be conceived in terms of temporal and material analogies. From this point of view the establishment of a monastery was like taking out an insurance policy. The church became the family mausoleum, and special masses were said there for the benefit of the founder's soul. The benefactor entered into a special relationship with the saint to whom his foundation was dedicated, and whose presence was represented by the relics contained in the altar of the church. Given the habit of thinking of human society as a hierarchy of feudal obligations, the saint in question was expected, in return for the dedication, to guard the interests of his mortal client in the world to come and at the Day of Judgment.

26,34

25. **The Last Supper,** and **The Washing of the Feet.** From the Perikope Book of Henry II (Clm. 4452). Early 11th century. 10¼ × 7½ in. (26 × 19 cm.). Staatsbibliothek, Munich. This book of extracts from the Bible, given by Henry II to Bamberg cathedral, is an example, like the contemporary but very different Sacramentary (plate 14), of an aspect of Ottonian art that was to be of importance in the development of 12th-century Romanesque painting. Compare the way in which the actions of the solid figures are emphasised here by the contrasting simple background, with the narrative style of the Albani Psalter (plate 48).

Not everyone was in a position to promote his eternal prospects by the expedient of founding a monastery. For lesser men there remained the consolations afforded by the holy places and the relics of the saints. In the curiously 20 practical way in which medieval men regarded their religion, some of the spiritual merit of holy men was held to have rubbed off on the localities in which they lived their lives and on their possessions, and in particular to have survived their deaths in the sense of adhering to their mortal remains. From these merit was given off almost like a gas, strong near the source, and weaker at a distance. To get the full benefit of relics it was therefore necessary to enter their physical proximity. This was done either by bringing the relics to those who wished to venerate them, or by sending the latter to the relics. Both were practised during the 10th, 11th and 12th centuries. In the nature of the case the acquisition of relics was liable to involve unedifying transactions. Claims to ownership were often disputed and ended in prolonged litigation. On the other hand pilgrimages as penitential exercises were popular with both

26. **Nave of La Trinité, Caen.** Second half of the 11th century and early 12th century. William the Conqueror and his wife founded the monastery of St Etienne and the nunnery of La Trinité at Caen to atone for their marriage as cousins. This early example of 'thick-wall' construction (see p. 100) was built with a vaulted choir, but the nave was only given its sexpartite vault (one of the earliest examples of this kind of rib vault) in about 1120, when the clearstorey windows received their present form.

Church and laity. It was inevitable that Jerusalem and the Holy Land should hold a unique place in the estimation of pilgrims. But the hazards and the length of the journey were sufficient to deter all but the most determined, and accordingly suitable alternatives were recognised at Rome or Monte Gargano in Italy, at Santiago de Compostela in north-western Spain and at several places in France, of which some at least were en route to Rome or Santiago.

The gross superstition of these attitudes was compatible with prodigious displays of fervour. A truly awe-inspiring feudal gangster, Fulk Nerra (Count of Anjou 987–1040), founded two abbeys himself, was closely connected with the origins of two more, and when he died, presumably in the odour of sanctity, was on the way back from his third pilgrimage to Jerusalem. Nor was this kind of piety at all feigned. If it made little difference to the conduct of their lives, it nevertheless betrayed a lively awareness of God's presence in the world and the dues that were owed to him by men of substance and position. The revenue necessary to maintain a community of monks, canons or nuns in the manner of life to which by 1050 they had become accustomed represented no small proportion of the total wealth at the disposal of society. Pilgrimages were less costly, but even so not everyone could incur the expense.

All this represented on the part of secular society a growing respect for the Church. That this was so was due in the last resort to the efforts which the Church itself made at the time to live up to its own pretensions. This brings us to the second great preoccupation of the 10th and 11th centuries—the reform movement in the Church. First and foremost, there was the recognition of abuses and corruption. Primitive societies, among which catastrophe is always imminent and frequently experienced, never fail to attribute their misfortunes to the wrath of God and presume that this animosity has been aroused against them by their own sins and shortcomings. The endless onslaughts of Vikings, Hungarians and Saracens from outside Europe, and the ever present chaos of feudal warfare within, provided plenty of scope for this kind of reflection, especially during the first part of the 10th century. The secular priesthood in particular came in for criticism. Too often it was tarnished by the sins of simony and incontinence, and a worried laity was apt to enquire whether the sacraments themselves were compromised by the shortcomings of the men through whom they were administered. The Church was unanimous in pronouncing that this was not so, but prudent men betook themselves to the discipline of monastic life just in case. The numbers, social importance and wealth of the postulants made monasticism for a time a major factor in European life. For two hundred years

27. West tower of La Charité sur Loire. 12th century.
The single surviving west tower of La Charité sur Loire, one
of the daughter monasteries of Cluny, is covered with a
profusion of ornament typically Burgundian in detail
(compare Autun, figure 40). Mature Romanesque
architecture often concentrated on elaborate surface
decoration applied to basically simple architectural forms.
Compare the earlier tower at Cluny (figure 28) and the
early Gothic towers of Laon (figure 86).

28. Ruins of the abbey church of Cluny. Late
11th and early 12th centuries. This tower and transept
are all that remain of the great abbey church begun in
1088, the third to be built at Cluny. The vast building
originally included towers above both its crossings and over
the double transepts, as well as at the west end. The idea of
multiple towers goes back to Carolingian buildings and
continued into early Gothic architecture (see figures 20, 86).

(c. 950–1150) monks were a sort of spiritual *corps d'élite*,
responsible by the purity of their lives and the rigour of
their observance for procuring the goodwill of God toward
Christians in general and specific benefactors in particular.

Between the interests of the laity, often anxious to
control monasteries for their own purposes, and monks
anxious to escape the contagions of worldliness, frictions
and disagreements were always possible. Already in the
10th century the desirability from a spiritual point of view
of emancipating monasteries from excessive interference by
secular benefactors was recognised. Cluny was one of the
first fruits of this more enlightened outlook. Duke William's
foundation charter formally eschewed all rights and reservations on the part of the founder and his family, and the
only external authority which Cluny was obliged to
recognise was that of the Pope himself. In the course of the
10th century, under a succession of distinguished abbots,
Cluny rose to a position of eminence among the monasteries
of Europe. If the modes of observance practised there were
not exactly those envisaged by the rule of St Benedict or
the Desert Fathers, the pomp, dignity and elaboration of
its liturgies set an exacting standard which its neighbours
found expedient to emulate. Cluniac monks were invited
to reform the customs of other Benedictine foundations. At
first these benefits were gratuitous, but by the time of the

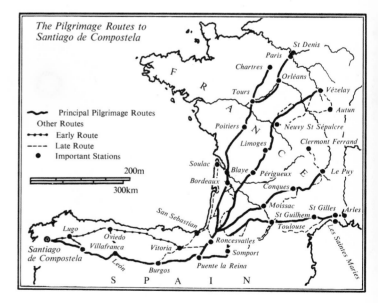

29. The main routes used by pilgrims to the shrine of
St James at Santiago are known from a 12th-century
'guide book', but it would appear that the routes were already
well established by the second half of the 11th century, when
most of the great pilgrimage churches were begun. (See
plate 21, figures 32, 33.)

28

fourth abbot, Odilo (994–1049), Cluny was in a position to embark on a policy of direct annexation. Gradually a kind of monastic empire was built up—an ecclesiastical counterpart to the secular immunities of the feudal dynasts. This vast congregation created a precedent which other religious orders such as the Cistercians followed in the 12th century. And to some extent the Church as a whole did likewise, especially in its dealing with secular governments; it tended to behave like a privileged organisation exempt from the normal obligations of political obedience.

As a corporate embodiment of ecclesiastical power Cluny was certainly exceptional, but as an instrument of Church reform it was only one among several contemporary movements. In the Low Countries and what was then called Lotharingia, similar efforts were made to restore the life of the Church in accordance with its pristine standards; and under the influence of Cluny and Lotharingia monastic life was revived in southern England during the late 10th century by St Dunstan, St Ethelwold and St Oswald. The Lotharingian movement, unlike Cluny, was concerned with the secular clergy. Moreover its point of view was to a much greater extent determined by the doctrines of early canon law, in which the status of the Church as a divinely instituted body was set forth with admirable clarity, undimmed by any serious consideration of what was likely to happen if these high-flown claims were actually implemented. This was the intellectual background of the men who purged the Church of its abuses and set it in what they conceived to be its rightful position, beyond all secular control at the apex of human society. The culmination of the movement was the reform of the Papacy itself during the middle years of the 11th century. The success of this operation led to a head-on collision between the Church and the secular powers, involving what the latter regarded as vested interests hallowed by tradition. The issue really turned on who should control the assets of the Church—the ecclesiastics themselves or their lay patrons. There were political overtones as well. But overall the Church made a determined and fairly successful bid to take charge of its own resources; and in spite of bitterness and the conflicts which arose, there is little doubt that society was persuaded to accept the Church as its own ideal aspect.

It is necessary to dwell at some length on these matters, and to stress the variety—even the inconsistency—of the attitudes involved, for without them it is impossible to understand what the Romanesque revolution was about. The great churches, monumental sculpture, metalwork and new styles of painting were part of a vast effort in which the whole of Christendom tried to get its values sorted out. What began in the 10th and 11th centuries was one of those deep-rooted and spontaneous urges on the part of society as a whole to come to terms with the higher aspects of human life, which up to then it had been content to neglect. Unlike the Carolingian renaissance, which had been the precarious achievement of a few high-minded scholars, inspired by an almost ludicrously unreal vision, this movement was broadly based on the genuine aspirations of Christian folk. Whether they realised it or not, they were setting out to become civilised, and in this respect Romanesque Europe resembled nothing so much as archaic Greece.

The fact that from the end of the 11th century Romanesque art and architecture were designed almost exclusively as propaganda to project its own exalted image on the world was not inconsistent with these wider and vaguer implications. On the contrary, in order to construct prestige buildings here on earth worthy of the Church Triumphant architects were called upon to tackle structural problems that had not been faced since late antiquity and, to find solutions, they were forced to look far beyond the horizons of their previous experience. In the same way, as men thought more deeply about the symbolism of the Church, new decorative ideas came into vogue, and new problems arose in the representation of the human form, which launched the more adventurous artists on courses that opened their eyes to the achievements of classical figure art.

ROMANESQUE ARCHITECTURE

To begin with the architecture. In any precise sense of the word, there is no such thing as a Romanesque style of architecture. Thanks to the combination of feudal patronage and the aspirations of the reformed Church, more churches were built, and more of them were bigger churches. Moreover the bigger churches tended to become more elaborate in both plan and structure. But given the local character of feudal life, church building was largely conducted on a regional basis. Neighbours took their standards of economy or magnificence from one another. The same group of masons could therefore spend their whole working lives producing similar buildings all within a hundred miles. So the Romanesque architecture of Burgundy is different from that of Normandy, and it is possible to identify distinctive Romanesque schools in Provence, Auvergne, Alsace and western France, not to speak of the local differences that occur in England, Spain and Italy. It is true that special circumstances such as Imperial patronage in Germany or the successful promo-

(Continued on page 65)

20 (opposite). **Statue-reliquary of Ste Foi.** Head, 5th century; statue, last quarter of the 9th century, modified during the last quarter of the 10th century. Plates of gold and silver gilt over a wooden core, with precious stones, cameos, enamels, etc. h. 33½ in. (85 cm.). Church of Ste Foi, Conques. The statue was originally made to house the relics of Ste Foi, which were brought to Conques between 864 and 875. From 985 onwards the relics became celebrated for their miracles, and many additions were made to its ornamentation in the subsequent centuries. (See p. 65.)

21 (opposite). **Nave of St Sernin, Toulouse,** looking east. Late 11th–12th century. St Sernin at Toulouse, one of the main centres on the road to Santiago, has the long barrel vaulted nave, tall arcades and spacious galleries typical of French and Spanish pilgrimage churches (see p. 65). The east end was consecrated in 1076 but the plainer nave was completed

in brick only during the course of the 12th century.

22 (above). **Golden altar from Basle** (detail). Before 1019. Gold, precious stones, pearls. 47¼ × 69¼ in. (120 × 177 cm.). Cluny Museum, Paris. Given by Henry II to Basle cathedral, this splendid altar frontal with its figures

in high relief standing beneath arches (an arrangement which goes back to Early Christian sarcophagi) reflects a growing interest in the use of the arch— not only in architecture (see p. 68) but also as a frame for figure sculpture (compare plates 36, 43, and figure 39).

23. Nave of Notre Dame la Grande, Poitiers, looking east. First half of the 12th century. This 'hall church' type of building, with aisles and nave of equal height, lit only by windows in the aisle walls, is characteristic of west French Romanesque architecture, but also became internationally popular in the Gothic period (see St Sebaldus, Nürnberg, figure 84). The painted decoration is 19th-century but probably gives some impression of the wealth of colour intended by the Romanesque builders.

24 (opposite). **Nave of S. Miniato, Florence,** looking east. 12th century. This splendid interior displays the Italian love of richly coloured building materials (see p. 73). An interest in surface decoration rather than in structural innovation is typical of Tuscan Romanesque architecture: this building is basically a wooden-roofed basilica in the Early Christian tradition, though with the innovation of a choir raised above a spacious crypt, the Italian alternative to the east end with subsidiary chapels (see figure 32 and p. 66).

25. **Detail of wall-painting in the church of S. Angelo in Formis.** Late 11th or early 12th century. Precise links between the art of the East and Western Europe are surprisingly difficult to determine. This painting may reflect the style that flourished nearby at Monte Cassino, where Abbot Desiderius had many contacts with the East. But whether the Byzantine elements in this work, which appear less transmuted than in other Romanesque painting (compare plates 31 and 49), derive directly from contemporary metropolitan Byzantine art or from lost Italian intermediaries remains uncertain.

26 (opposite). **Christ in Majesty.** Detail of painting in the apse of the chapel at Berzé la Ville, Burgundy. Early 12th century. The chapel at Berzé la Ville belonged to St Hugh, abbot of Cluny. It seems likely that it was decorated before his death in 1109 by artists from the great abbey, and thus gives some impression of the kind of monumental painting that existed at Cluny itself. (See also plate 28.)

27. **Cefalù cathedral,** Sicily, from the
south-east. Begun 1131. The Norman
conquest of Sicily resulted in the
absorption of some architectural ideas
from northern Europe into a country with
an already mixed culture. While the
interior of this building contains pointed
arches of Muslim type, and has mosaics in
the Byzantine tradition, the general plan
and the use of decorative intersecting
arches can be paralleled in earlier
examples of Anglo-Norman architecture.

28 (opposite). **Apse of the chapel at
Berzé la Ville,** Burgundy (reconstruction
in the Palais de Chaillot, Paris). Early
12th century. Berzé la Ville (see also
plate 26) is one of the few surviving
examples of an apse still completely
covered with Romanesque painting of
high quality. The vault shows *Christ in
Majesty* surrounded by the apostles, with
figures of saints below, depicted in a
wealth of colour not often found in
Romanesque wall-painting. (Compare
plates 29 and 31.)

58

29 (opposite, above). **The Crossing of the Red Sea** (detail). Wall-painting in church of St Savin sur Gartempe. *c.* 1100.

30 (opposite, below left). **St Paul and the Viper** (detail). Wall-painting in chapel of St Anselm, Canterbury cathedral. Late 12th century.

31 (opposite, below right). **St Michael.** Wall-painting in Le Puy cathedral. Late 11th century or early 12th century. The fragmentary survival of Romanesque wall-painting makes it very difficult to understand the stylistic and iconographic development of this type of art. The monumental figure of *St Michael* at Le Puy (plate 31) shows in its rather crude detail some echo of the stylistic conventions of Byzantine art (compare plate 25), while the detail from the extensive cycle of Old Testament scenes at St Savin (plate 29) perhaps has more in common with Carolingian and Ottonian traditions of narrative painting (compare figure 25). The much later painting of *St Paul* at Canterbury illustrates the close connections that can exist between wall-painting and book illumination— compare the treatment of the drapery with that in the Bury Bible, plate 49 (see p. 80).

32 (right). **A Prophet.** Stained glass window in Augsburg cathedral. Early 12th century. This window with the figure of a prophet, one of five in the west end of Augsburg cathedral, is one of the earliest surviving examples of a complete stained glass window, and shows that the art was already highly developed. Theophilus, writing in the early 12th century, refers to the practice of placing brightly coloured figures on a ground of white glass. (See p. 74.)

33 (above left). **The Crucifixion.** Stained glass window in
Poitiers cathedral. Mid-12th century.

34 (above right). **The Ascension.** Stained glass window in
Le Mans cathedral. Mid-12th century. As windows became
larger during the 12th century, elaborate stained glass
compositions tended to replace single figures (compare plate 32).
These two examples from west France, with their stylised
gesticulating figures, belong to the traditions of late
Romanesque painting and metalwork (compare plates 49, 51)
which continued side by side with the development of early
Gothic architecture.

35 (opposite). **The Virgin and Child.** Stained glass window in
Chartres cathedral. Late 12th century. The reused glass of this
magnificent window in the ambulatory at Chartres, traditionally
called the 'Belle Verrière', is of an earlier date than the
13th-century medallions that fill most of the other windows.
The glowing reds and blues that dominate the composition are
typical of stained glass of the early Gothic period.

62

36 (left). **Detail of carved slab from St Sernin, Toulouse.** Late 11th century. Marble. The original function of this figure carved in high relief, one of a series (see also figure 8) now in the ambulatory of St Sernin, Toulouse, is uncertain. It illustrates the revival of interest in large-scale stone sculpture in late 11th-century France; its style shows a close dependence on late antique work, still commonly found in southern France.

37 (below). **Four apostles.** Wall-painting in S. Clemente, Rome. 12th century. This frieze decorates the apse of the upper church of S. Clemente, Rome, which was built above the Early Christian basilica. Like the sculpture at Toulouse, it is in a style strongly reminiscent of the art of the Early Christian period.

38 (opposite). **West front of Verona cathedral.** Mid-12th century. The projecting porch and lion supports are characteristic of the developed Italian Romanesque west front. The small figures placed against the angles of the jambs show the increasing desire to integrate figure sculpture with its architectural setting, which led ultimately to the fully developed 'column figure' (see p. 78, figure 52).

30. Interior of Notre Dame du Port, Clermont Ferrand,
looking east. 12th century. The decoration of the interior of
this building with local stone, and the plan, similar to that of
the pilgrimage churches but with four instead of five radiating
chapels, are features typical of Auvergne Romanesque. A
central octagonal tower surmounting a lofty crossing which is
abutted by the raised inner bays of the transepts is also a
design peculiar to this region.

31 (below). **Crypt of Worcester cathedral. Begun 1186.**
Worcester was one of several English churches built soon after
the Conquest with a crypt of considerable size. Note the
typically 11th-century groin vaults and undecorated cushion
capitals. The popularity of both cushion capitals and large
crypts in post-Conquest architecture suggests connections with
the Empire as well as with Normandy, where these features
are less common.

, 29, 32, tion of international pilgrimages could result in the wider
33 diffusion of more ambitious types of building. Essentially,
however, the architects of the 11th century were concerned
with the appropriate form for a great church, and it is this
preoccupation rather than any particular solution that
gives unity to Romanesque architecture.

In the treasury of the church of Ste Foi at Conques in
Auvergne, the principal attraction is a little jewelled
20 statuette purporting to represent the lady to whom the
church is dedicated. This image was made about 980, and
for such an early date it is an exceptional object. It is a kind
of reliquary, and one may guess that it acquired a human
form because a late Roman bronze head was fortuitously
available. This gruesome little figure is hardly a work of
art, but it conveniently displayed the things of real value at
Conques, which drew pilgrims from hundreds of miles
away—the relics of Ste Foi. These were responsible for the
miracles which in turn were the source of a considerable
part of the abbey's income. Together with benefactions,
they made it possible by the middle of the 11th century for
the abbey church to be rebuilt on the scale that we see
today.

32 This church at Conques was one of a group which share
21 the same basic design. Others are at Toulouse (St Sernin)
and Santiago de Compostela in Spain. Two more, at
33 Limoges and Tours, were destroyed after the French
Revolution. Although they were exceptional buildings and
are not to be thought of as 'typical' Romanesque churches,
they illustrate several important and characteristic trends.
First and foremost, as they were all concerned with the
display of relics to pilgrims, special care was lavished on the
part of the building in which these were housed, the
east end. Formerly it was the practice in churches which
possessed valuable relics to conceal them underground in
crypts, and to make access to them as difficult and in-

39 (opposite). **Cloister of Monreale cathedral.** Late 12th
century. Stone with mosaic glass. While the cloister of Monreale
cathedral, built by the Norman William II, has pointed arches
with flat geometric inlaid decoration reflecting Muslim
influence, the style of the capitals, like so much Mediterranean
Romanesque sculpture (compare plate 24, figure 50), shows the
strong influence of classical prototypes, a mixture typical of
Sicily (compare plate 27).

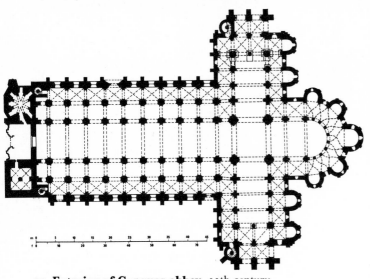

32. **Exterior of Conques abbey.** 11th century.

33. **Plan of St Martin, Tours.** 11th and 12th centuries.
The 11th-century church of St Martin at Tours was possibly the prototype for the developed 'pilgrimage church'—no two of which, however, are quite identical. The ambulatory and ring of chapels became a standard feature, but the completely aisled transept and towers of Tours were not always copied. Conques, begun before 1065, is less ambitious than the larger later churches at Toulouse and Santiago (see plate 21).

convenient as possible. Relics were treated as a kind of buried treasure. This was no doubt prudent when danger threatened. But with the reorientation of the Church's relations with the secular world, relics were so to speak brought out into the open, and presented to the world at large. Where there was no crypt, the reliquary was displayed on the altar. Otherwise the crypts themselves were enlarged so that instead of dark and narrow passages they became veritable halls spread under the choirs and *31* transepts of churches. This solution was favoured in Italy and the Rhineland. But either way the change involved a radical departure from the traditional types of church design. At Conques and kindred buildings the east end is particularly elaborate. It is often said that the semicircular ambulatory around the apse of the choir, and the series of chapels opening radially from it, which we find there, were designed to solve problems arising from processions, etc. This may well be true. But the significance of the ambulatory was not exhausted by considerations of convenience. In Early Christian times it had been the practice to construct special churches, usually centrally planned, for relics and the services devoted to their veneration. These were usually adjacent to but separate from the great halls, or basilicas. In the pilgrimage churches these two early types of church were combined into a single unified design.

34. Interior of Fontevrault abbey, looking east. Early
12th century. A number of large west French Romanesque
churches in the area of Angoulême and Périgueux are vaulted
with a series of domes—an idea that must be inspired by
domed buildings of the East. Fontevrault, a northern outlier
of this group, was the burial place of the Plantagenet kings
of England, who ruled so much of western France.

35. Interior of St Martin du Canigou, looking west.
11th century. This small church in the Pyrenees is an example
of one of the early completely barrel vaulted buildings that
are to be found particularly in Italy, Spain and southern
France, where so many examples of Roman vaulted buildings
survive.

The tendency to merge two historically distinct types of
church was a special case of another, more widely spread
practice, namely that of stressing the contrast between the
two ends of the church. Although the Church was an
organisation that embraced both clergy and laity, and
although both frequented the same buildings, nevertheless
the reform movement tended to accentuate the gulf
between them, and the parts of church buildings which
they respectively used often received different architectural
emphasis. Thus the east end which was reserved for the
clergy, and which contained the principal altars and
reliquaries, was now habitually more elaborate than the
nave. The ambulatory and radiating chapel plan was one
way of stressing the importance of the east end. It was
particularly effective from the outside, where the various
32 roof levels could be made to ascend stage by stage to reach
their climax in a central tower. It is unlikely that the sense
of hierarchy which we still detect in the east ends of these
churches was unintentional. Another method was to put a
35,36 vault over the choir. The introduction of stone vaulting was
partly encouraged by the need to protect altars and
reliquaries from the dangers of fire from a wooden roof; but,
like central planning, vaults had iconographical overtones
which contributed to the symbolism of church architecture.
All vaults could symbolise the vault of heaven, and had

done so long before Christianity adopted the idea for its
own purposes. From this point of view the vault *par excellence* was the dome, which in so far as it approximated to
part of a sphere could claim to participate in the perfections
of that most perfect of all Platonic shapes. Domes were
habitually used in Byzantine churches and for a time also in
certain parts of France. The difficulty with domes, however,
was that they did not readily lend themselves to use in
longitudinal churches (nor in aisled churches) which by *34*
tradition most Western churches were. These difficulties
could be overcome, and the results were often strikingly
effective. But by and large other solutions were preferred.

VAULTS AND ARCHES

So far as the Middle Ages were concerned, all vaults came
from Rome, and apart from domes the other Roman types
available were the barrel vault and the groined vault. *38*
Barrel vaults were easier to construct and accordingly the
first to be tried. They were first used over choirs, as at
Agliate near Monza in Lombardy. Then they were
extended to the whole church, which is what happened at
Conques. A whole tradition of Romanesque church
building developed around the barrel vault. The surviving *21,35,36*
monuments are to be found from northern Italy to the *56*
Atlantic coast of France and Spain. We have only to put,

36. **Interior of St Philibert, Tournus,** looking east. 11th and 12th centuries. This impressive 11th-century nave was vaulted in the 12th century in an unusual fashion with a series of barrel vaults supported on transverse arches set at right angles to the main direction of the building. Transverse barrel vaults had already been used in the aisles of the early 11th-century narthex.

37. **Detail of the narthex, St Benoît sur Loire.** 11th century. St Benoît sur Loire has an 11th-century narthex with groin vaults separated by arches, which spring from piers with attached half columns—an early example of the compound pier, which becomes a basic feature in developed Romanesque architecture. Note the variety of Corinthian and historiated capitals—some of the earliest French examples of elaborately carved capitals.

for example, Notre Dame la Grande at Poitiers or S. Martín at Frómista near Burgos alongside the ruins of the classical Roman nymphaeum at Nîmes to realise how direct was the descent of southern Romanesque architecture from the traditions of antiquity.

Medieval groined vaults also seem to have started from Italy. Presumably there were still examples of late Roman vaults of this kind in cities such as Milan or Ravenna which had Imperial associations. There were certainly some to be seen in Rome itself. It was, however, in the north of Europe that the possibilities of this kind of vaulting were most thoroughly explored. Groined vaults are really only suited for use over square or nearly square compartments; and a whole series of 11th- and 12th-century churches in Lombardy and the Rhineland seem to betray in their planning care to make provision for this necessity. Even so, the geometry of their construction was liable to seem complicated and almost from the start we find a tendency among the designers of vaults to simplify their procedures by substituting straightforward arches for the more sophisticated curves of true groins. Once this step had been taken it required little further imagination to stress these by making them visually conspicuous. The result was the kind of vaulting which is called the ribbed vault.

Because ribbed vaults became an essential feature of Gothic architecture, some historians have had a strong inclination to distinguish this kind of vaulting from the use of groins. However, one is only a refinement of the other, and both developed in the context of Romanesque architecture. Enough has been said elsewhere about the struc-

tural convenience which ribbed vaults offered, but other factors were involved as well. However else they were regarded, ribs soon come to be considered as arches, or parts of arches. One of the most widespread features of Romanesque churches, in every part of Europe, was the part that arches came to play in their general articulation. In Early Christian and Carolingian churches the only arches worthy of the name were to be found in the main arcades between the nave and aisles, where they were supported by columns or piers. Windows and doorways were often no more than holes, left unmoulded and undecorated. It is the application of colonnettes, capitals and moulded arch forms to these apertures which most commonly distinguishes a Romanesque church from its predecessors. During the 11th century we find the same form applied wherever possible to the articulation of the interiors of churches, so that by about 1100 a great church was well on the way to becoming an organised system of interrelated arches. The introduction of arches into the vaults of these churches was therefore just another instance of something that had already been going on for some time. It happened to require greater audacity, and the resulting effects were more conspicuous, providing as they did a certain vertical accent in the space that they covered.

What was the purpose of all these arches? Clearly the majority of them, especially those around windows and doorways, were primarily decorative. But we can go further than this. Arches like vaults had a symbolic significance for the Middle Ages. Set over or around the figures of saints, as for instance on the golden altar frontal

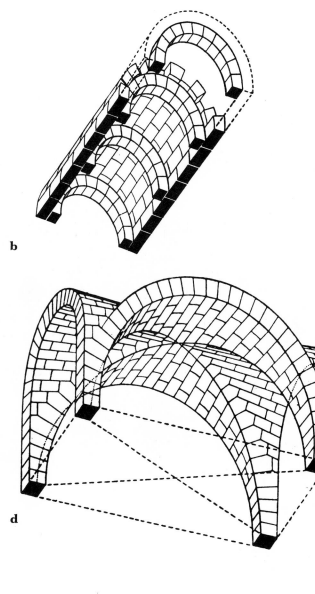

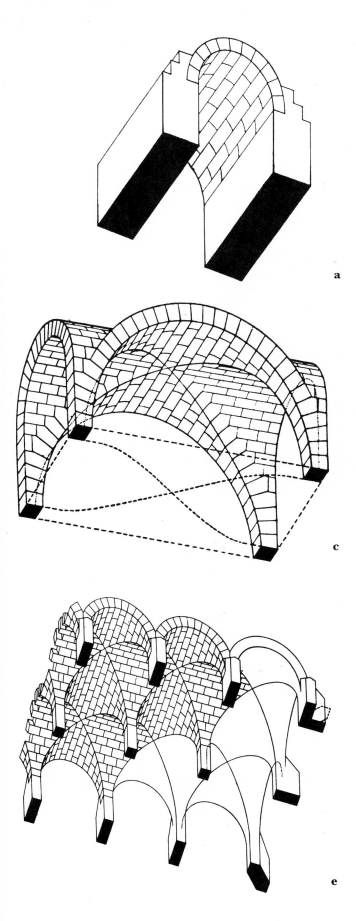

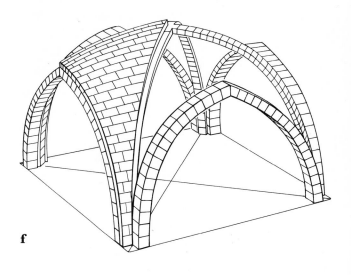

38. **Vaults.** The simplest kind of longitudinal vault is that
represented in figure (a), i.e. a long barrel vault. In
Romanesque churches this was usually combined with
transverse arches as in (b); a groined vault started
from the intersection of two barrel vaults (c). Unless both

barrel vaults were identical in span (e), the groins
themselves tended to undulate and the next step was to
'straighten' the groins into simple curves (d). The final step
was the substitution of arches, i.e. ribs, for the straightened
groins (f).

39. **West front of Notre Dame la Grande, Poitiers.** Mid-12th century. The application of sculpture to the whole façade is a feature typical of Romanesque architecture of west France, as is the absence of west towers. In this region figure sculpture is often used for entirely decorative purposes, particularly for the embellishment of arches, but in this building it is unusually prominent.

40 (opposite, left). **Nave of Autun cathedral.** Second quarter of the 12th century. Autun has the pointed arches, barrel vault and classical details such as fluted pilasters that are typical features of Burgundian Romanesque architecture, probably inspired by Roman remains. The main features of this building derive from the slightly earlier great abbey church at Cluny.

41 (opposite, right). **Detail of the west front of St Gilles du Gard.** 12th century. With its rather disorganised wealth of classically-inspired sculpture, this façade is a striking contrast to contemporary developments in northern France.

from Basle cathedral (now in the Cluny Museum in Paris), they conveyed the idea of victory in much the same way as Roman triumphal arches, and by an easy extension they came to represent the architectural abode of the Church Triumphant, i.e. St Augustine's *City of God* or the Heavenly Jerusalem. All through the Middle Ages churches, that is the actual physical masonry, evoked thoughts and images along these lines. But with the construction of the great churches of the Romanesque period, the imagery became particularly rich and vivid. Everything connected with these buildings was designed not just to impress people with the irresistible majesty of the contemporary Church Militant here on earth, but to bring about a direct confrontation between the faithful and the illustrious Christians of the past. To go into church was meant to be a foretaste of Paradise, where the distinction between the living and the dead was for a moment obliterated and men could really believe that they were participating in the Communion of Saints. The proliferation of arches in church buildings, irrespective of whether they served a structural or a decorative purpose, was part of a process whereby the church became a more comprehensive and satisfactory image of the heavenly mansions. Other aspects of the same process were the intensification of surface ornament, and the practice of inhabiting selected parts of great churches, such as the doorways and windows, with figures of saints, etc., and narrative scenes, to which we shall return later. But it is perhaps worth mentioning here that from this point of view there was no essential line of demarcation between the Romanesque and Gothic versions of the con-

cept of the great church. Both were preoccupied with the same fundamental symbols, and Gothic was only a more thorough-going and systematic presentation of the Romanesque iconographical programme.

Churches with articulated walls, arcades, doorways and windows, not to mention vaults, required masonry of a higher quality than had sufficed in earlier times. The 11th century saw the introduction of ashlar for church architecture all over Europe. (In certain places the need for stone castles intensified the demands on the quarries. Some of them, e.g. those near Caen, acquired an international reputation.) At first, cut stone tended to be used to augment rubble masonry at those crucial points where mouldings were required, around windows and doorways; but gradually ashlar either replaced rubble altogether, or else formed a kind of skin on either side of a rubble core. The latter method was particularly popular in Normandy and in England after the Conquest, and the walls so built tended to be very thick, and to require more extravagant articulation than walls elsewhere. This in turn led to a host of interesting developments that spread over into the Gothic period. But either way, the mere fact that great churches were henceforth built of stone forced architects to study the techniques of stonemasonry wherever these could be found.

First and foremost this meant referring back once again to antiquity. Vaults were not the only forms that the Romanesque Middle Ages derived from Roman architecture. Piers and elevations were likewise inspired. Several Carolingian buildings are known to have made specific

allusions to one Roman prototype or another, and in the Ottonian period the same thing happened. For Otto the Great's own cathedral at Magdeburg (*c.* 968) marble shafts were brought from Italy, as for the chapel at Aachen. The giant arcades of the basilica at Trier again exerted their influence—on the nave of St Pantaleon at Cologne (*c.* 955), and later on the cathedral of Speyer (*c.* 1030). The climax of this trend was reached at the end of the 11th century, when Speyer was drastically remodelled for Henry IV. This time Lombard vaults were added to the transepts and nave, and a series of remarkable Corinthian capitals gave the church a strong Imperial flavour. Outside Germany Roman forms seldom carried precisely the same significance. The most curious instance was the third abbey at Cluny, started about 1088. Here, when the building was complete, a visitor entered the precincts of the monastery through an imitation of one of the Roman gates at Autun, and the abbey church itself through a doorway decorated with sculpture that was set in a way recalling Roman or early Byzantine usage. The interior vistas vied both in size and actual arrangement with the largest of the Early Christian basilicas in Rome, old St Peter's and S. Paolo fuori le Mura, and the piers and upper walls were covered with fluted pilasters or half-columns, surmounted by Corinthian capitals. The allusions to Rome, whether classical or Christian, were too numerous to be explained as general symptoms of the age. Cluny seems to have been a deliberate retort to the classicism of Speyer. Some Church leaders clearly felt that the Pope was the true Emperor and that if there was to be any revival of classical forms it should

be conducted under the auspices of the Church. On the whole, however, this attitude was not widespread. It is true that in Burgundy itself and the Rhône valley a whole school of Romanesque grew up under the influence of Cluny; and near the mouth of the Rhône the west façade of St Gilles du Gard, ostensibly based on the *scaena* of a classical theatre, perhaps reflects similar sympathies. But it may be suspected that its fondness for classical details was one of the aspects of Cluniac art of which St Bernard so loudly disapproved, and under his influence the unsuitability for Christian churches of what soon came to be regarded as pagan forms was widely admitted. Nevertheless it was impossible for the building industry to proceed at all without making some references to Roman practice. Mathematical rules of thumb are a case in point. And at the visual level itself it would seem that, providing the allusions were unobtrusive enough, no objections were raised. For instance, if the nave of Tournai cathedral calls to mind the Pont du Gard, this is because Roman aqueducts in general suggested an appropriate method of procedure for constructing elevations in tiers of arches, not because one particular monument of this kind was endowed with special meanings for Church patrons. Many other allusions to aqueduct architecture can be detected in Romanesque churches, but elsewhere they are usually less obvious than at Tournai.

It is the same with compound piers. Square piers with engaged half-columns are liable to occur almost everywhere in Romanesque churches. Ultimately they must be derived from classical Roman prototypes which may be

represented by the piers of the Colosseum. This derivation is particularly apparent when the medieval examples include Corinthian capitals, whether newly cut or reused. Nevertheless Romanesque compound piers always make sense in terms of the visual logic of the design of which they form a part. There was no antiquarianism for its own sake. On the contrary, contemporary problems were being solved by the intelligent use of an antique convention; and if, as often happened, this required the original to be modified, even drastically, no one appears to have lamented the ensuing deformities. The same practical consideration which made it necessary to refer to antiquity in the first place nearly always tempered respect for what was found there.

LINKS WITH THE EAST

On occasion, in fact, Romanesque architects were prepared to look beyond Rome, and even beyond Byzantium, for the inspiration they required. It is becoming increasingly apparent that there were great numbers of disconcerting links (mainly dating from the 11th century) between the Romanesque architecture of western Europe and the Christian architecture of Armenia and Georgia. Just why there should be these links between the two extremities of Christendom is something of an historical puzzle. They were certainly already there before the Crusades began, and it is doubtful whether the journeys of individuals (mainly religious) could account for the surprisingly technical similarities that we encounter. On the whole we are forced back to quite general reflections. The only considerable part of the Early Christian world which developed a church architecture in stone was around the eastern Mediterranean, more especially in Syria. After the loss of Syria to the Muslims in the 7th century this particular architectural tradition seems to have survived in the moun-

42 (opposite, above). **The Pont du Gard,** near Orange.
1st century AD. This is the most outstanding surviving example
of Roman aqueduct construction, consisting of superimposed
tiers of arches. Compare this technique of building with the
cathedral of Tournai (figure 43).

43 (opposite, below). **Nave of Tournai cathedral.** First
half of the 12th century. Tournai cathedral is one of the few
surviving examples of a number of influential churches built
in the 12th century in the wealthy towns of this border area
of the Empire. The use of coloured marble and the
reduction of the wall surfaces by four storeys of arches were
ideas taken up in the early Gothic architecture of northern
France (see figure 42).

44. **Nave of Salisbury cathedral.** Second quarter of the
13th century. Salisbury cathedral was begun on a new site in
1220. The use of Purbeck marble, the lancet windows and the
relatively low height in comparison with contemporary
French buildings, are typical of the 'Early English' period of
English Gothic, which lasted until the rebuilding of
Westminster abbey in the mid 13th century introduced
England to the latest French ideas.

tainous regions of eastern Anatolia, and as soon as the West
began to develop a stone architecture of its own, the ob-
stacles evidently were not of an order to prevent the flow
of ideas from East to West.

One of the circumstances that may have favoured this
improbable traffic was the power and prestige of the
Byzantine Empire. At the turn of the millennium, the real
centre of civilisation was still the Middle East where, in
spite of the religious conflict between Christian and
Muslim, some sort of cultural continuity—and in the case
of Constantinople political continuity as well—had been
preserved with the classical past. One way of regarding the
Romanesque period in western Europe is as a gigantic
effort to catch up with the Greeks and Arabs; and although
relations were bedevilled by suspicion, prejudice and
ignorance on both sides, it was to the Mediterranean, and
the lands beyond the Mediterranean, that the northerners
constantly turned for instruction and guidance.

It was this orientation toward the south and south-east
that gave Italy its unique status in the Romanesque world.
Not only did it contain in Rome the religious capital of
Latin Christendom, but it was the only country of the West
which still retained considerable traces of its classical past,
both in art and in learning. Moreover it pointed like a
finger toward those regions where higher standards of
civilisation were recognised, and although Italy was no
longer the political centre of gravity in the West, ideas and
forms passed through that country as through a funnel, on
their way to north-west Europe.

The Italians made their greatest impact on the north in
the field of decoration rather than in the construction of
churches. Apart from vaults, which for iconographical
reasons were of interest to everybody, and where the
Italians got a head start thanks to the particular richness of
their inheritance from Rome, their views on how churches

should look were too much determined by local considerations to have any close bearing on northern problems. The
Early Christian churches of Italy exercised a constant if not
easily specified influence over later medieval architecture
there. The great basilicas, with their long rows of fine
marble columns, represented a norm from which patrons
were always reluctant to move away. In the cathedral of
Pisa, in S. Miniato at Florence and more or less everywhere
south of Rome there seems to have been an incredibly
plentiful supply of antique columns waiting to be used in
11th- and 12th-century churches. Abbot Desiderio had
some brought to Monte Cassino, and sets of them, not
always matching, are to be found in nearly every Romanesque church in Sicily and Apulia. This Italian predilection
for marble columns did occasionally penetrate into the
north. Abbot Suger at St Denis wished to follow Desiderio's
example in his new choir (1140); and the much extolled
beauties of the choir of Canterbury in the 12th century
must also have included some coloured marble shafts. The
northern centre from which this taste disseminated was the
Low Countries, where a suitable supply of dark marble
was discovered early in the 12th century near Tournai. But
it lasted longest in England, where Purbeck marble shafts
continued in use until the 14th century.

COLOUR IN BUILDING

The use of coloured marble slabs as revetments for brick
or concrete was an Imperial Roman practice, continued
through the most expensive strain of Early Christian and
Byzantine churches. In conjunction with mosaics on the
upper walls and vaults, it produced effects of the utmost
splendour. The basic idea behind this kind of church was
that of the audience chamber of an Imperial palace, over
which Christ himself, the Pantocrator, presided like an
Emperor on his tribunal. Very few Western churches ever

45. **The Agony in the Garden.** Mosaic in Monreale cathedral. Last quarter of the 12th century. Monreale, founded by William II in 1174, was, like other Sicilian churches, decorated in the Eastern fashion with mosaics. These represent the type of artistic style derived from Byzantium which may have been familiar to northern artists such as Villard d'Honnecourt, possibly through the medium of pattern books. (Compare plate 53, figure 62.)

commanded the resources necessary for this sort of decoration, and the mere fact that Latin churches were designed in a totally different way from the Greek type made it impossible for the complicated schemes of Greek iconography to be transferred to the West without being drastically modified in the process. The Royal Chapel at 45 Palermo, the cathedral of Monreale, and St Mark's in Venice, the three outstanding instances where serious attempts were made to carry out the Greek programme, were all the result of direct contact with Constantinople itself (see *The Early Christian and Byzantine World*). Nevertheless, the palatial and sumptuous interiors of the Early Christian and Byzantine tradition acted as a kind of yardstick against which Romanesque ingenuity measured 28 itself in emulation.

The normal counterparts of mosaic in the West were painting and stained glass. Not one of the great original schemes of Romanesque monumental painting has sur- 29 vived intact, unless the Genesis cycle at St Savin is placed in this category; the interest of that, however, is more iconographical than stylistic. Occasionally, as at S. 25, 26, 28 Angelo in Formis not far from Naples, or at Berzé la Ville near Cluny, we have fairly extensive cycles which may be presumed to follow closely in both form and content the examples of their more illustrious neighbours (in these cases, respectively, Monte Cassino and Cluny itself). But by far the greater part of the Romanesque wall-painting known to us has survived for reasons that have little or nothing to do with its quality. Some, notably in England, has been protected by later paint, plaster or whitewash, and some in out of the way places like the valleys of Catalonia have remained untouched because money has never since been available to improve on them. Painting was so easy, cheap and convenient that it must have been the most universal form of embellishment in Romanesque

churches. Yet one cannot escape the feeling that it occupied the lowest place in the decorative hierarchy, and that wherever possible more expensive media would have been preferred. If they could have used mosaic, they would most certainly have done so. The materialism of the Middle Ages is nowhere more apparent than in its rating of the arts according to the costliness of their ingredients. Compared with gold, ivory or marble, even the rarest pigments were outclassed. To be fair, however, this attitude must not be confused with the vulgar venality of the traditional bourgeoisie of later times. Substances had symbolic, even mystical, properties not far removed from magic. Moreover, colours were seldom at their most intense when spread over the vast surfaces of church walls. This aspect of Romanesque art—its love of deep, strong or strident colours—found its most authentic expression in stained 35, 44 glass and enamels, rather than in painting, properly so-called. And when painting did achieve something like the brilliance of jewellery or enamels this was usually in the field of manuscript illumination. Occasionally, however, we encounter fragments of wall-paintings such as the monumental *St Michael* at Le Puy, or the exquisite *St Paul* 31, 30 at Canterbury, whose outstanding quality compels us to wonder what riches have been lost.

Stained glass is an art form so closely associated with Gothic architecture that we are apt to forget the extent to which it must have been exploited in Romanesque times. Yet it is evident that Theophilus, the author of the treatise *De Diversis Artibus* written in Germany during the first half of the 12th century, knew recipes for coloured glass that went back long before his own time, and claims have recently been made that Carolingian fragments still exist. So perhaps the secrets of the late Roman glass-makers of the Rhineland were never entirely forgotten by their Frankish successors. Be that as it may, when Abbot Suger 3 wanted glass-painters to make new windows for St Denis in about 1140, he was able to recruit them '*de diversis nationibus*' ('from various peoples')—which implies that skill in the art was already widespread. One place where stained glass may have been used before St Denis is Canterbury, which was extolled by William of Malmesbury for, among other things, 'the light of its glass windows'. The frames of some of these still survive and are curiously uneven as though they were deliberately designed for the glass they contained, and this would hardly have happened if the subject-matter had not been important. As with so many other aspects of Romanesque art, one is tempted to locate the centre from which glass-painting spread across Europe in the Mosan area, although apart from Augsburg most of the early windows that have actually survived are in France, at St Denis itself, at Chartres, Le Mans and Poitiers.

ROMANESQUE SCULPTURE

Whatever innovations are to be found in the Romanesque handling of colour, these were at least accomplished within the context of a living tradition. Monumental sculpture, however, had to be more or less recreated. For this reason it has perhaps come to be regarded as the Romanesque art form *par excellence*. Certainly it is the one that conforms most readily to modern notions of what art should be. Historically speaking, however, the contemporary vogue for Romanesque sculpture is apt to be misleading. What we tend to like about it now has very little to do with the purposes and aspirations that it set out to fulfil. In the wider context of medieval art as a whole, Romanesque sculpture betrays the uncertainties of men who had no clear idea of what could be done with their new medium. Local schools were formed, each with their own pattern-books and stylistic formulas, but these gave way to one another with bewildering rapidity. For some, impossible movements conveyed the violence of divine inspiration—as for instance the *Isaiah* at Souillac. Others, like Gislebertus of Autun, contrived to evoke the pathetic helplessness of humanity, caught up in the toils of an inexorable fate. Within three generations of its inception the art had already changed out of all recognition, and within two more (at least in France) it had entirely ceased to have any connections with its Romanesque origins.

In many ways, the progress of Romanesque sculpture from the late 11th century to the point in the middle of the 13th when it had become completely Gothic resembled that of archaic sculpture in Greece. Whatever else is involved, sculpture is concerned with the third dimension, and for medieval Europe, as for ancient Greece, the ultimate significance of the third dimension lay in the greater realism with which it allowed images to be endowed. At the end of the process, in both cases, we are left with what purported to be imitation human beings. In retrospect we are therefore entitled to say that the revival of monumental sculpture in the 11th century was the first step in the direction of a truly representational art, and that all the

46. **Isaiah.** Second quarter of the 12th century. Abbey church of Souillac. This expressive figure from a doorway is now reset with other fragments on the inside of the west door of the church. The style of this example of south-west French Romanesque sculpture derives from the important works at Toulouse and Moissac dating from the early 12th century.

marvellous patterns and stylisations that we admire so much and so rightly in Romanesque sculpture were blind alleys that led nowhere.

From this point of view the history of Romanesque sculpture was a quest for emancipation from the residual enchantments of older conventions that really belonged to the world of two-dimensional art. In one respect, however, Romanesque sculptors were in a different position from their Greek predecessors. Whereas the latter had to work out the formulas of ideal naturalism for themselves, the Romanesque had some of the achievements of classical antiquity to guide them. For them the problem was basically one of insight, sympathy and understanding—the finding of new uses for what already existed, rather than the invention from scratch of a new conception of art.

From among the cat's-cradle of interwoven themes which make up what we know of Romanesque sculpture, we may select two threads for guidance. In Italy, Provence and northern Spain, where classical Roman reliefs and statues were still to be seen in profusion, it is evident that Romanesque sculptors came under the influence of antiquity almost from the start. Thus recognisable references to late antique works that still survive are to be found at Toulouse before 1100. The outstanding figure in these early stages, however, was Wiligelmo, whose reliefs on the west front of the cathedral of Modena already show considerable awareness of what could be done with classical draperies. Even more unmistakably classical are the decorative reliefs on the main doorway of Modena cathedral which show little naked figures climbing through luxurious vine scrolls. The best classical instances of this particular motif are to be found at Leptis Magna in North Africa, but the same kind of thing must have been plentifully represented in Italy, perhaps even at Modena itself.

In the north of Europe, on the other hand, classical

remains were far fewer in number and far less inspiring in quality. Here it seems to have been a general practice for would-be sculptors to take their patterns and subjects from the nearest available paintings. These were usually, though not always, to be found in the illuminated manuscripts in the library of the church that was being decorated. Thus it is clear that the men who carved the capitals in the crypt of Canterbury cathedral were familiar with the ornamented initials that were painted in the adjacent scriptorium. And the patterns that we find carved on the jambs and arches of Romanesque doorways like those at Paray le Monial and Chartres were taken from the painted columns and arches that framed the canon tables of early gospel books. One can imagine that before there was any carving at all in northern churches some forms had simply been painted on the surface of the masonry and, when carving began, its purpose was simply to throw these patterns into greater relief.

But sculptors very soon found themselves confronted with problems peculiar to their own art. In the first place the surfaces that were destined for sculpture, namely capitals, and the tympana and recessed jambs of doorways, were uncongenial in shape and placed at inconvenient angles. The virtuosity with which they applied themselves to the solution of these problems still evokes our admiration. Nearly all the well known works of Romanesque sculpture are reliefs, superbly adjusted to the overriding conditions of the parts of the buildings to which they were assigned. It is from this that we derive our vivid sense of integration between architecture and sculpture. The figures are not just added; they seem to grow out of the masonry. It is not a question of their inhabiting so much as animating the structure. And this, fundamentally, is what they were intended to do—to turn a mere building into a living image of the Church. Through their iconography they were in

8, 49

36

50

41, 46,
48, 49,

47 (opposite). **Gislebertus.** *The Damned.* Detail from the west tympanum, Autun cathedral. Second quarter of the 12th century. Some of the most impressive Burgundian Romanesque sculpture is to be found at Autun (see figure 40) where the splendid Last Judgment tympanum is signed by the sculptor Gislebertus—an unusual feature for this century when most art is anonymous. (See also p. 7.)

48. **The Apocalyptic Vision.** Tympanum of the abbey church at Moissac. First third of the 12th century. The relatively few Romanesque tympana which are on this exceptional scale are mostly to be found in Burgundy and south-west France. This awe-inspiring vision of Christ surrounded by the evangelists' symbols and the Elders of the Apocalypse skilfully fills the entire available space. Compare the contorted figures and the agitated crowding of forms with Chartres west front, only a few decades later (figures 51, 60).

49. **Lintel at St Genis des Fontaines.** 11th century. The lintel of this Pyrenean church is carved in low relief with figures beneath arches whose horseshoe shape suggests the influence of the Muslim art of Spain. An inscription gives the date of 1020–1. A carved lintel was one of the simplest forms of architectural decoration; later Romanesque doorways became increasingly elaborate (see figure 51).

50. **Capital from Toulouse.** Late 12th century. Musée des Augustins, Toulouse. This double capital, probably from a cloister (compare plate 39), is carved with motifs directly inspired by antique art, although the way they are skilfully arranged to fit the form of the capitals is typical of the Romanesque style. It was this kind of subject-matter that inspired the polemics of St Bernard (see p. 98).

fact able to do more. By carefully matching themes from the Old Testament against the Nativity, the Passion of Christ, the life of the Virgin and the prophesied events at the end of time, they contrived to present both the Church's view of world history and its own role in world history.

But it was precisely this purpose that impelled the sculptors to explore the possibilities of the third dimension, and their really outstanding achievement lay in their ability to conceive their figures more and more in the round. From this point of view the presence of so many shafts and arches in northern Romanesque churches was to prove decisive. By and large, the idea of applying monumental sculpture to buildings spread from south to north. One of the places where it developed most rapidly was in doorways, where for instance in the chapter house of the cathedral of Toulouse (c. 1130) statues were placed obliquely across the jambs of the recessed entrance. In the south we can trace this development typologically if not chronologically from flat reliefs like those on the piers of the cloister at Moissac (c. 1100) to what we find in the cloister piers at St Trophime, Arles (c. 1170), where statues are placed across the corners. From this sort of thing, which was no doubt done on many occasions before Arles, it is but a short step to the Toulouse doorway; and if intermediaries are required, they may be found in the small jamb figures of the doorways of the

38 cathedrals of Verona and Ferrara in Italy (c. 1135–40).

When these ideas reached the north the practice of articulating doorways and windows with engaged or even free-standing shafts was already well established. The problem of applying figure sculpture to doorways therefore resolved itself into the improbable task of carving a figure in relief on a column. In the nature of the case such reliefs tended to become figures in the round, and it is fascinating to trace the gradual metamorphosis of these figures into fully rounded free-standing statues. In the Royal Portal at Chartres (c. 1150) we can see how in the early stages incredible efforts were made to preserve the architectonic character of the column. Later at Senlis (1170s) the figures

52 began to move; at Chartres again (after 1200) they began to turn; and by the time we get to the north transept of

63 Reims (c. 1220) they have virtually detached themselves from the building altogether. Smaller figures were applied in much the same way to the roll mouldings that framed the

52 arches over the doorways, and they likewise gradually emerged into fully three-dimensional forms.

63 At Reims the statues have already acquired something more than a superficial classicism. It would be wrong to suppose, however, that the stone carvers had found their own way back to antiquity unaided. During the last quarter of the 12th century spectacular steps in this direction had been taken by a celebrated Mosan metalworker

64 called Nicholas of Verdun. In the great enamelled altarpiece that he made for the abbey of Klosterneuburg near

65 Vienna (c. 1180), and even more obviously in the Three Kings shrine of Cologne cathedral (c. 1200), Nicholas reveals a deep understanding of the conventions of classical

51. **The Entry into Jerusalem.** Capitals on the west front of Chartres cathedral. Mid-12th century. On the doorways of the west front of Chartres (which are earlier than the rest of the building) the sculpture is spread over all available areas—lintels, tympana, voussoirs, jambs, columns and capitals—to form an elaborate iconographic programme (see also figure 60). Note how the capitals form a frieze which can depict a whole Biblical narrative.

52. **Melchizedek, Abraham, Moses, Samuel, David.** Column figures on the east side of the central porch of the north transept of Chartres cathedral. First quarter of the 13th century. When Chartres cathedral was rebuilt, the west front was retained, but elaborate new portals were constructed at the end of each transept. These monumental Old Testament figures, in spite of their relative naturalism in comparison with Romanesque versions of the same theme (see figure 46), appear, however, stiff and elongated when compared with the roughly contemporary sculpture of Reims (figure 63).

53. **Roger of Helmarshausen.** *Portable altar from Paderborn.* 1100. Silver, precious stones, pearls. 6¾ × 13¾ × 8¼ in. (17 × 35 × 21 cm.). Cathedral Treasury, Paderborn. This altar was made at Helmarshausen for Bishop Henry of Werl by an artist named Roger in 1100.

The linear modelling of the lively apostles is a remarkably early example of an artistic technique that recurs throughout the 12th century in painting and metalwork and even occasionally in sculpture (compare plates 49, 51).

drapery, and even to some extent the relation between drapery and the underlying physical anatomy. His faces also remind us of classical as well as Byzantine types. No doubt Nicholas was a remarkable innovator, but it is no accident that these developments should have taken place in the context of metalwork rather than stone sculpture. The whole order of procedure was different. Once the practice of beating strips of metal over wooden cores had been left behind, and casting became prevalent (after 1150), the formative stages in figure design were done by modelling as opposed to carving. As was the case in antiquity itself, this particular method of creation always seems to have allowed greater scope for movement and gesture, and the miniature scale on which they habitually worked also encouraged the more uninhibited metalworkers to show off their talents. Long before Nicholas of Verdun these symptoms had shown themselves in other virtuosi such as Rainer of Huy or Godefroid of Claire. When Theophilus wrote his treatise on the arts, he assumed that the same craftsman would be called upon to draw and paint illuminated manuscripts, to make glass and enamels and to work precious metals. Stone carvers were odd men out in this company, offshoots of the totally different trade of masonry. In one sense what happened during the 12th century is that the sculptors in stone broke away from their parent body, the masons, and moved over into the camp of the image-makers. But the latter themselves did not remain static. Until not long before the time of Theophilus the arts of which he wrote were either two-dimensional or else conceived in low relief. They consisted essentially of the application of colour or a little modelling to preliminary drawings, and the drawing styles in question were still derived from the great continuous tradition of medieval drawing going back to late antiquity, which is most fully represented for us in manuscript illumination. By the end

of the 12th century, however, emphasis had shifted in an entirely different direction. If painters and metalworkers still shared a common drawing style in 1200, this was now derived from another source altogether, namely the drapery conventions of classical sculpture. In other words, at some point in the 12th century, initiative in drawing seems to have passed from a two-dimensional art to a three-dimensional one. From this moment on, the various forms of painting fell more and more under the influence of metalwork and sculpture. This is not to say that painting at once set out to imitate the three-dimensional effects that were natural to sculpture, although in the long run this is exactly what happened. To begin with, it was more a question of painters producing two-dimensional abstracts of figures meant to be seen in the round—as though painters actually used drawings intended for the preparation of sculpture. We can see this perhaps most clearly if we compare the Ingeborg Psalter at Chantilly with the drawings by Villard de Honnecourt who was a mason, and the statues in the north transept portals at Reims.

53
62
89

DRAWING AND PAINTING

But the process must have begun long before this. One of the ways in which we distinguish a Romanesque manuscript from its predecessors is by the firm smooth lines of the drawing. There is all the difference in the world between the feathery calligraphy of Anglo-Saxon outline drawings and, say, the great *Christ in Glory* of the Stavelot Bible, or the solemn hieratic figures of the St Albans Psalter. No doubt this is making the point in the crudest possible way, but it seems obvious that a fundamentally new concept of the function of drawing is part of what we mean when we talk about the Romanesque style in manuscript illumination. This new drawing style uses line in much the same way as a glass-painter or an enameller would—to indicate precisely

22, 23
47
48

and clearly the boundaries of colours, not to hint vaguely at an impression of movement, or to convey the agitation of feeling. It represents in fact just those affinities which Theophilus postulates in his treatise. Let us take another case. In all the great English bibles of the middle years of the 12th century, Bury St Edmunds, Lambeth and Winchester, there is to be found a very characteristic drapery convention known as the 'damp-fold' style. This consists essentially of double sinuous lines that run over limbs in a way that suggests their corporeality. It is, however, not confined to manuscript illumination. It occurs in the *St Paul* at Canterbury, and on metal objects like the Warwick ciborium. And in fact it would seem to have originated in metalwork before it was taken up by the painters. There is a famous portable altar at Paderborn which was made at the very beginning of the 12th century, in which the damp-fold is present, or at least distinctly anticipated. The author of this work was Roger of Helmarshausen, who may well have known Theophilus, or may even have been Theophilus.

When we turn from drawing to colour, the same sort of conclusion is forced upon us. It is perhaps ridiculous to generalise, but if there is any characteristic Romanesque taste in colour, it is for the deep, rich tones. The light washes that tint Anglo-Saxon outline drawings eventually go the same way as the drawing style itself (although not without putting up a tremendous resistance). We can see the process at work very clearly in the succession of copies that were made in England of the Utrecht Psalter. In the Anglo-Saxon version (Harley MS. 603, British Museum) all the fundamental characteristics of the original are preserved. In the mid 12th-century version, the so-called Eadwine Psalter at Trinity College, Cambridge, the kinship can still be recognised, although there is a perceptible ossification in the outlines. In the last version, however, the Paris Psalter, dating from the end of the 12th century, everything has changed. Both drawing and colour have hardened, and if it were not for the more or less identical iconography we would scarcely admit that the manuscript belonged to the same family. In the case of manuscripts the fact that alternative styles were available allowed considerations of expense and economy to come into play, and for this reason alone purely stylistic trends are more difficult to trace. Nevertheless, where cost was no object, as for instance in the Winchester Bible, a definite predilection may be observed for strong and vivid colours which approximate, as far as the medium will allow, to the brilliance of stained glass or enamel. These latter, of all the arts concerned with colour, were the ones most dear to the hearts of Romanesque patrons. Enamelling was in fact more or less perfected during this period. The addition of a translucent glaze to an intensely coloured piece of metal, however small, epitomises what was perhaps the most deeply felt of all the aesthetic urges of the High Middle Ages in the West—the sense of almost mystic awe in the presence of jewellery. From this point of view enamelling

was in a way the nearest they came to Byzantine mosaics. This is probably the basic reason for their great preoccupation with Byzantine forms during the middle years of the 12th century, although the mere fact that the Middle Ages approached classical antiquity from a background of abstract and heavily stylised art would make Byzantium an almost ideal intermediary.

The upshot of this survey of the relations between the various arts of western Europe during the 12th century is that metalwork occupied a central position of crucial importance. We talk of metalwork as an art, but for the Middle Ages what gave metalwork its significance were the purposes it served, i.e. the objects it made. Of all the arts it was the one physically most closely associated with the things that really mattered—the altars and reliquaries of the great churches. The relationship was reciprocal. Some of the holiness of the contents passed to the containers and, to be worthy of what they held, the sacred vessels had to be made of the most precious materials. Given the distinctive mood of Romanesque religiosity, its superstition and its sense of pomp and hierarchy, this distribution of emphasis within the arts was inevitable. Only architecture, which in Romanesque terms served exactly the same purpose, namely that of housing relics, albeit on a different scale, could sustain an equal status. All the rest, however beautiful and expensive they may have been, were ancillary.

The realisation that churches and reliquaries were fundamentally the same thing was one of the great Romanesque discoveries, and it continued to be one of the cornerstones of the Gothic art which followed. Very few of the great reliquary caskets which were made in the 12th century have survived; and, of those that do, not one can truly be said to have the form of a building (except the little domed structures either brought from or made under the direct influence of Byzantium). But just as churches themselves became more and more elaborate systems of arches, and were increasingly possessed by visible reminders of sacred events, analogies and personalities, so also were the reliquaries. The two forms gradually grew towards one another; and if the final identification did not take place until Gothic times, this is yet one more pointer to the conclusion that there was no real break or line of demarcation between the two styles. Until we really get down to details, Romanesque is in many ways simply incomplete Gothic.

(Continued on page 97)

40 (opposite). **The Gloucester Candlestick.** 1104–1113. Bell metal. h. 23 in. (58 cm.). Victoria and Albert Museum, London. Identified by an inscription as having been made for Gloucester abbey at the instigation of Abbot Peter, whose rule therefore dates the candlestick. It has recently been assigned to a workshop closely associated with the Canterbury manuscripts.

41. **Rainer of Huy.** Baptismal font (detail). 1107–1118. Cast bronze. h. 25 in. (64 cm.). Church of St Barthélemy, Liège. Commissioned by Hellinus, whose presence at Liège was first mentioned in 1107, the font itself was described in 1118. Rainer of Huy was the first of the great 12th-century Mosan metalworkers whose names have come down to us. The font is remarkable for the classical quality of its figures, a characteristic of the Mosan school which becomes even more obvious in the work of Nicholas of Verdun.

42. **Workshop of Egbert of Trier.** Reliquary shrine of the foot of St Andrew. 977–93. Gold, ivory, enamel, precious stones, etc. h. 12¼ in. (31 cm.). Trier cathedral. This reliquary belongs to a widespread group in which a piece of a real arm or foot is kept in an imitation arm or foot. This practice may be ultimately of Irish origin.

43. **Gable end of the Shrine of Heribert.** Third quarter of the 12th century. Copper gilt, silver gilt, enamel, filigree, precious stones, rock crystal. 26¾ × 16½ in. (68 × 42 cm.). Heribert church, Deutz, Cologne. The elaborate decoration of this large coffin-sized reliquary in all kinds of metalwork techniques demonstrates the important role of the shrine in the medieval church (see p. 80). In all types of metalwork (as in churches) in the 12th century, an increasing use is made of figures in relief (see also figures 39, 75).

44 (opposite). **Plaque from the tomb of Geoffrey Plantagenet.** Third quarter of the 12th century. Champlevé enamel. $24\frac{3}{4} \times 13$ in. (63 × 33 cm.). Musée Tessé, Le Mans. This plaque with a prince in ceremonial vestments from the tomb of Geoffrey Plantagenet, originally in the church of St Julien at Le Mans, is an unusually large example of the type of richly coloured enamel-work produced in the Limoges region in western France. Limoges enamels became very popular, especially in the 13th century, when they were widely exported.

45 (right). **Enamelled cross.** Mid-12th century. Copper gilt, precious stones, enamel. Musées Royaux d'Art et d'Histoire, Brussels. The champlevé enamels on this cross, typical examples of 12th-century Mosan work, depict Old Testament events prefiguring the Passion of Christ—for example (lower scene) the cross-like mark made with the blood of the Passover Lamb (Exodus 12). This use of Old Testament 'types', very common in the decoration of liturgical objects, also occurs in paintings, sculpture and glass (see plate 57).

46 (below). **Charlemagne dedicates Aachen minster to the Virgin.** Relief from the Charlemagne shrine, Aachen. Early 13th century. Silver gilt, copper gilt, enamel, filigree, precious stones. Aachen minster. The ceremonial translation of the relics of Charlemagne to this shrine, in the presence of Frederick II in 1215, was not simply a religious gesture, but a deliberate political move by the German ruler to counter the growing cult of Charlemagne as the founder of the French monarchy.

47 (above left). **The Master of the Majesty of Christ.** *Christ in Majesty*. 1093–7. From the Stavelot Bible (B.M. MS. Add. 28106–7, f. 136r). 17¼ × 10¾ in. (44 × 27 cm.). British Museum, London. The Master of the Majesty of Christ was one of the decisive contributors to the formation of the Mosan style, which emerged in the period about 1100 at Liège and the group of important abbeys in the vicinity. The plasticity at which the miniaturist aims has a close analogy with metalwork (see the font of Rainer of Huy, plate 41).

48 (above right). *Entry into Jerusalem*. First half of the 12th century. From the Albani Psalter (f. 19r). 11 × 7¼ in. (28 × 18 cm.). St Godehard, Hildesheim.

49 (left). **Master Hugo.** *Moses and Aaron*, and *Moses and Aaron numbering the People*. Mid-12th century. From the Bury Bible (frontispiece to the Book of Numbers, f. 70r). 20½ × 14 in. (52 × 36 cm.). Corpus Christi College, Cambridge. The Albani Psalter (so called from its supposed connections with St Albans, though in fact it belonged to the nearby nunnery of Markyate) is prefaced by a series of full-page illustrations of the life of Christ in a style which, with its monumental, solidly modelled figures set against a simple coloured background, suggests links with both Ottonian narrative traditions (figure 25) and the new developments in Mosan art (plate 47). The profound influence of the Albani master on English painting, hitherto dominated by the delicate drawing style in the tradition of the Utrecht Psalter (figures 22, 23), can be seen in the slightly later great Bible from Bury St Edmunds, but here the rather subtler modelling becomes in places almost abstract patterning. (Compare plates 30, 34, 50 and see p. 80.)

50. **Wall-painting in St Sepulchre chapel, Winchester cathedral.** 12th and 13th centuries. Beneath this early 13th-century Gothic wall-painting of Christ lie the remains of some late 12th-century work close in style to one of the artists of the Winchester Bible. The difference between the two works, probably only a few decades apart, exemplifies the rapid changes of style that took place at this period.

51. **The Master of the Leaping Figures.** *The Egyptian smiting the Hebrew* and *Moses slaying the Egyptian*. Second half of the 12th century. From the Winchester Bible (historiated initial at the beginning of the Book of Exodus). Winchester cathedral. The Winchester Bible, one of the large illuminated Bibles made in England in the 12th century, was illustrated by several artists, probably for St Swithin's priory, Winchester. The way in which the work of the Master of the Leaping Figures, so called because of his love of agitated movement, contrasts with the mentality found in the Bury Bible (plate 49), despite the similarity of drapery conventions, illustrates the diversity of mature Romanesque style.

52 (above left). **'He that walketh uprightly, and worketh righteousness...'** *c*. 1200. Detail of a page from Paris Psalter (MS. Lat. 8846, Psalm 15, f. 23r). Bibliothèque Nationale, Paris.
53 (above right). **The Agony in the Garden.** *c*. 1200. From the Psalter of Queen Ingeborg (MS. 1695, f. 24v). Musée Condé, Chantilly.
54 (left). **Doubting Thomas.** From the Gospels from St Martin, Cologne (MS. 9222, f. 98v). First quarter of the 13th century. Bibliothèque Royale, Brussels. These three illustrations exemplify the crucial departure from the traditions of Romanesque painting (compare plates 49 and 51) that took place around 1200, and must reflect the influence of the metalwork of Nicholas of Verdun (figures 64, 65). The Psalter made for Queen Ingeborg (plate 53), like the drawings by Villard d'Honnecourt (see figure 62), shows particularly clearly the preoccupation with a figure style deriving its inspiration from antique sculpture, which is also to be seen in contemporary work in both stone and metal (plate 70, figure 63). The later, rather more fluid and dramatic style of the Gospels from Cologne (plate 54) shows the interpretation of these ideas in Germany (compare it with the Gothic sculpture at Bamberg and Naumburg, plates 71 and 73). The radical nature of the change from Romanesque to Gothic can hardly be better illustrated than by the Paris Psalter (plate 52) which, though following the iconography of the Utrecht Psalter (figure 22), is in a style completely different both from the latter and from its 12th-century copy.

55 (opposite). **Chalice.** *c*. 1140. Sardonyx, and other precious stones, metals, etc. h. 7½ in. (19 cm.). Widener Collection, National Gallery, Washington. One of Abbot Suger's principal treasures. It was lost in 1804, but reappeared in 1922. The sardonyx cup is made from a single stone, which impressed Suger very much. The base is much restored.

56 (left). **South transept of Noyon cathedral.** Third quarter of the 12th century. Noyon cathedral, begun slightly earlier than Laon (compare figure 61), is constructed with a basically 'thick' wall (see p. 100) which is hollowed away by a series of openings and passages, particularly apparent in this south transept end where there are no chapels or galleries to block the light. This concern with lightening the mass of the wall is one of the driving forces behind the development of early Gothic architecture.

57 (opposite). **'William the English-man'.** *Ambulatory of the Trinity chapel, Canterbury cathedral,* looking east. Late 12th century. The east end of Canterbury cathedral was rebuilt after a fire in 1174, in order to provide a lavish setting for the shrine of St Thomas à Becket. With its use of coloured marble shafts and columns, its large stained glass windows (see also plates 63 and 64) and its foliage capitals, it is one of the earliest examples of the influence of early Gothic ideas outside France. (Compare figures 59, 71.)

58 (opposite). **Inner aisle of Bourges cathedral.** End of the 12th and early 13th centuries. The 'échelon' arrangement of the elevation of Bourges cathedral makes it possible for the main nave, the tall inner aisles and the lower outer aisles all to be lit directly. This complicated system was not widely imitated. (See also plate 59, p. 111.)

59 (above). **Ambulatory of Bourges cathedral,** looking east. Late 12th and early 13th centuries. The spacious ambulatory of Bourges is still lit by its original stained glass. The sequence of the ambulatory windows is only broken briefly by the very small projecting chapels, which themselves each have three windows. The way in which the Bourges architect achieved his lighting effect (see also plate 58) was quite different from the contemporary solution of Chartres (see p. 109). It was the latter, however, which became the classic formula for the High Gothic cathedral (compare figures 73, 77).

60 (right). **Interior of León cathedral,** looking east. Third quarter of the 13th century. León cathedral, with its walls almost entirely filled with tracery windows, is a direct transplantation to Spain of French Gothic ideals of the mid 13th century (see plate 61). Compare the lighter effect of the glass here with the deep colours of the earlier glass at Bourges.

61. **Nave of Troyes cathedral,** looking east. Mostly 13th century. Begun in the early 13th century but completed rather later, Troyes cathedral, with its delicate tracery windows and glazed triforium, reflects the influence of the 13th-century work at St Denis (see figure 77). The uninterrupted vaulting and the similar subdivision of triforium and clearstorey give the nave walls the screen-like unity that becomes a typical feature of late Gothic architecture (see figures 78, 81).

62. **Vaulting in the ambulatory of Sta Maria del Mar, Barcelona.** Begun 1328. This building, perhaps the greatest achievement of Catalan Gothic, was substantially completed by 1384 when the first mass was held at the new altar. The spacious dimly lit interior is in complete contrast to León (plate 60) and its French preoccupation with light.

63. **Samuel,** and **Noah.** Stained glass in Canterbury cathedral. Late 12th century. The clearstorey windows of the new choir of Canterbury (see plate 57) were originally each filled with an Old Testament figure, illustrating the genealogy of Christ, while some of the ambulatory windows had related Old and New Testament subjects. Many churches must have had similarly elaborate iconographic programmes, which have been lost because of the fragmentary survival and frequent resetting of so much medieval glass.

MINO DESPERATVS SCVTB INVOCAT

Gothic Art

In or about 1135 Abbot Suger started to replace the decayed Carolingian fabric of his abbey church at St Denis, outside Paris. The fame of this new building rests perhaps more firmly on the reiterated publicity that Suger himself gave it, rather than on the actual innovations that were incorporated into its design. Clearly, however, no expense was spared, and we may therefore be certain that it was both as resplendent and as up-to-date as it could be made. The work fell into two quite separate campaigns—one beyond the west end of the old church, and the other beyond its east end. It was not until the middle of the 13th century that the resulting fragments were joined together, and then it was on a scale and in a style quite different from anything Suger had envisaged.

At the west end Suger planned a monumental façade with two towers and three doorways. There is a considerable body of evidence to suggest that these doorways were among the first in northern France to have the sculptured jambs and voussoirs that subsequently became obligatory for all churches with any pretensions to be considered important. So one might have expected that Suger would at least have mentioned the sculpture. In fact he passes it over in unwonted silence, and this has led some writers to suppose that the sculpture was added after his time. Be that as it may, he does think fit to draw our attention to other features of the doorways, namely that some, if not all, of the doors were made of bronze, and one of the tympana above them was filled with mosaics. The bronze doors of St Denis anticipated by a decade those of Bury St Edmunds in England; and both sets must be regarded as remote representatives of a practice whose home was Italy even if the craftsmen who made them came from the Low Countries. Moreover the precedent for bronze doors in the West was set by no less a building than old St Peter's at Rome. So in this respect Suger's intentions seem to have been retrospective rather than forward-looking. In the case of the mosaics he admits that their use was 'contrary to the modern custom', and the same inferences can be made.

That Suger's aim was—in some sense of the word—to create an Italian church in France is most clearly revealed by his admission that at one stage during the rebuilding of the choir he actually contemplated having marble columns shipped to St Denis from Rome, just like Desiderio for Monte Cassino, and it was only the providential discovery of a quarry near Pontoise, where suitable alternatives could be got more cheaply, which deflected him from this purpose. It is in fact possible that some of Suger's sculptors came from Italy. There are reliefs on the doorways at St Denis which have a remarkable resemblance to similar works at Modena. But it is an open question as to whether they came direct, or via the Low Countries, along with Suger's metalworkers and (as seems eminently probable) his glass-painters as well. In view of the state of the evidence, this is a question which it is perhaps better to ask than to answer, but the implications are important and far-reaching. For what it is worth, we may recall that there was at least one church in the Low Countries, St Maria at Utrecht, which inside and outside was closely modelled on Italian designs, and it was built at almost exactly the same time as St Denis. It would of course be ridiculous to attribute everything in Suger's church to this one overriding consideration, but in so far as Italy and the Low Countries played a part in determining his views on the appropriate appearance and furnishing of a great church, St Denis falls into line with Canterbury, Bury and Lincoln in England, and reflects what in retrospect seems to have been the mainstream of Romanesque taste, rather than a new beginning.

It is necessary to state all this at the outset because there is a persistent and by now no doubt inextinguishable tradition that St Denis was the first Gothic church. In point of fact, there is nothing inconsistent about this claim if we are prepared to accept the view that Gothic was simply the continuation and fulfilment of certain tendencies already present in Romanesque art and architecture. When allowances have been made for what was orthodox and conventional about Suger's patronage, two features are left outstanding which call for comment. One is his attitude towards symbolism; the other is his architecture.

It used to be thought that Suger was one of the great in-

54. **Plan of the abbey church of St Denis.** Mid-12th century. Suger rebuilt the west end and the choir of the abbey church of St Denis, leaving the Carolingian nave and transept, which were not rebuilt until the mid 13th century. The east end was begun in 1140, after the west end was ready, and was consecrated in 1144. (See figures 55, 77.)

64 (opposite). **Stained glass in the Trinity chapel, Canterbury cathedral.** Early 13th century. Before the invention of tracery, large windows were subdivided by iron bars to support the glass, which was frequently arranged in a pattern of roundels, squares or lozenges. The Trinity chapel, Canterbury (see plate 57) containing the shrine of Thomas à Becket, was filled with glass illustrating his miracles; the reset roundel here depicts an unidentified figure calling on the saint for aid.

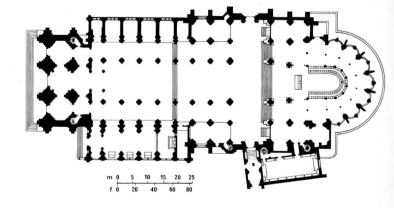

m 0   5   10   15   20   25
f 0   20   40   60   80

novators in the realm of iconography—for instance, that he invented the Tree of Jesse. We now realise that this was not so—indeed, that nearly everything which seems new in medieval imagery arose from more thoughtful reflection on perennial Christian themes. Nevertheless Suger broke new ground in the reasoned account—one is almost tempted to say defence—of symbolism that appears in his writings on St Denis. In this he was undoubtedly responding to the prevailing moods of his generation, to the intellectual as represented by Abelard, no less than to the puritanical as represented by St Bernard. Abelard was not directly concerned with the arts, although it is perhaps not entirely fanciful to detect an echo of his stringent standards in the careful visual logic of early Gothic architecture. But the formidable personality of St Bernard loomed large in Suger's affairs, and at one stage the two men virtually confronted one another over questions to which art was indirectly relevant. It is tempting nowadays to dismiss St Bernard as an insufferable bigot who disapproved of almost everything that everyone else liked, and with a flair for hectoring rhetoric which no one knew how to rebut. But by shifting the focus of Christian attention away from the material pomp of altars, reliquaries and church buildings to the spiritual condition of the individual soul, he gave a new depth to medieval religion at a time when it was an open

question in many parts of Europe whether the tremendous enrichment of human experience which the 12th century made possible would be kept within the traditional framework of Christianity. Though he was certainly no humanist himself, St Bernard's insight into what Christianity was really about played no small part in preparing the way for the humanism that was to come. From this point of view, his attacks on the indiscriminate ornament and visual seductiveness of contemporary Romanesque churches were entirely justified. With the scandalous behaviour of Pons de Melgueil known to everybody, it was very difficult to meet St Bernard's charges that Cluniac magnificence was born of the sin of pride and that it nourished pride in those who were surrounded by it. (Pons was abbot of Cluny from 1109 to 1122, and he had to be deposed for his excesses. On the death of his successor, he tried to recover Cluny by force. He failed, and ended his days in a Roman prison.) But the standpoint from which St Bernard mounted his attack on Cluny was a new one. He looked at church ornaments solely in terms of their effect on men, and from this point of view they could be regarded simply as distractions. No one made out a case in defence of the Cluniac position, but if they had done so it would probably have been along the lines that the right and proper way to honour God was to offer him the best that was available, that is the most expen-

55 (opposite, left). **Ambulatory of St Denis.** Before 1144. The skilful use of the rib vault over the awkwardly shaped bays of the double ambulatory, the slender monolithic columns and the large number of windows give this interior a light and spacious atmosphere that is strikingly different from earlier Romanesque buildings. (See p. 99.)

56 (opposite, right). **Interior of Fontenay abbey,** looking east. 1139–47. Early Cistercian architecture in France, of which this is one of the few surviving examples, took over the pointed arch and barrel vault from Burgundian Romanesque, but without the complicated plan, the towers and the elaborate decoration (compare figures 27, 28, 40) that were considered irrelevant to the principles of the new order.

55 sive and the most skilfully wrought things. The assumption that God would share their own delight in gold, jewellery and bright colours was no doubt primitive and naive. But the anthropomorphism was unconscious, and as an expression of religious feeling it was touchingly genuine, until questioned. Things were never quite the same after St Bernard and, although Suger's sympathies were all with the old-fashioned point of view, he realised that some sort of theological justification was henceforth needed for ecclesiastical iconography, and some degree of order and discipline to control its ramifications. Not that he set out to state his case systematically in the manner of the later scholastics. He found what he wanted in the writings of a Greek neo-Platonist, known as Dionysius the Areopagite, or Pseudo-Dionysius, who, though he lived in Syria in about 500 AD, was nevertheless confused or identified with the Dionysius who followed St Paul, and with the Dionysius, or Denis, who was the evangelist of the Paris region and titular saint of Suger's abbey. Between these writings and the predominantly Augustinian outlook of contemporary theologicans there was a fundamental kinship which guaranteed their respectability, while the special emphasis which they placed on the mystic role of light in human experience seemed to provide precisely the argument that was needed to allay the suspicions of St Bernard. In the event, Suger tightened up the discipline at St Denis, and he was allowed to carry out his artistic programme there unmolested. St Bernard turned his attentions to what he considered the infinitely greater danger of Abelard's rationalism.

Although it does not seem to have been an important part of Suger's case, it was inevitable that his more serious approach to church symbolism should carry didactic overtones, and from this point of view it is perhaps legitimate to place him at the beginning of a fruitful development. He was not, however, unique in his generation on this account. His contemporary Peter the Venerable, the abbot of Cluny who succeeded Pons, was very much of the same mind. In the last resort, Sugar's claim to be regarded as the father of Gothic rests on the somewhat fortuitous circumstance that

he happened to employ an architect of genius.

It was once remarked with considerable insight that in its early stages Gothic was the Romanesque of the Ile de France. During the 11th century, when great experiments in architecture were being made elsewhere in France, the region around Paris, though not wholly quiescent, played a relatively insignificant part. This was the one area of France ruled directly by the king, and perhaps nothing reveals more clearly the comparative weakness of the French crown at this stage of its history than its poor showing in the field of patronage when measured against the record of the feudal aristocracy elsewhere. With the rebuilding of St Denis all this was changed. A veritable flood of great buildings followed and, although few of them were the result of direct royal patronage, they faithfully reflect a momentous change in the fortunes and prestige of the French monarchy, a change for which Suger himself was in some measure responsible, in so far as he was the first of that distinguished line of French ecclesiastical statesmen who served their king perhaps even more zealously than their Church. Up to this moment, the Ile de France was a kind of vacuum, and the works at St Denis drew architects and craftsmen from all the regions around into a kind of melting pot. It is hardly surprising that a new style should have emerged from the fusion. But in order that it should do so, a masterful imagination was needed, and this was provided by the architect of St Denis.

It is probable that Suger's views about architecture were of a fairly general nature—that is, he wanted a sumptuous building and one that contained a large number of stained glass windows, prominently displayed, and beyond that he was prepared to leave the design to his architect. Clearly, great masses of masonry were inconsistent with these conditions, and if slender columns of marble were to be used they would not have to carry any great load. The clue to the solution of the problem was found in the ribbed vault. As we have seen, this was a structural device that had been developed in northern Italy at the end of the 11th century along with other varieties of vaulting, and from there it had passed, in ways that are not altogether clearly understood, to the Anglo-Norman kingdom that straddled the English Channel. The outstanding instance of their use in that part of the world was at the cathedral of Durham (1093–1133). It was suggested on p. 68 that the ribs themselves eventually came to be regarded as arches, different in function but not different in character from those which were placed around doorways and windows. Almost from the start this idea seems to have been present in Italy, but at Durham there are several features in the masonry which make it clear that the ribs were not conceived in an organic relation with their supports. They were simply arcs of stone, inserted where necessary to carry the broad surfaces of the vault. The great masses of masonry at Durham, i.e. the piers and walls, were still the primary structural elements and, although there were plenty of arches in the building, they were not related to one another in a systematic way.

55

57

57. **Nave of Durham cathedral,** looking east. Late 11th and early 12th centuries. The east end of Durham cathedral, begun in 1093, was designed with a vault, but the nave appears to have received its rib vault only after a change of plan. Note the great thickness of the walls, a typical feature of Anglo-Norman buildings (compare figure 26), and the chevron ornament which became a hallmark of English Romanesque decoration.

58 (opposite). **Galilee chapel, Durham cathedral.** Late 12th century. The Galilee chapel built on to the west end of the cathedral, with its richly ornamented arches resting on slender columns (before restoration there were two, not four columns, in each group), demonstrates the attenuation of mass associated with early Gothic architecture, but which is here found applied to purely Romanesque forms.

In this respect St Denis is perhaps closer to its Italian precursors; but the application of arch forms to masonry was such an Anglo-Norman speciality, and St Denis was in several other ways so closely connected with the architecture of Normandy and the Norman border, that it is perhaps easier to see it as a development from the Anglo-Norman tradition.

THICK-WALL AND THIN-WALL CHURCHES

The really crucial difference between St Denis and the great buildings of the Normans lay in the thickness of their respective walls. Moulded arches applied to masses eight feet thick could never be more than a special kind of surface decoration. But to the east and south-east of Normandy there appears to have been during the 11th century no decisive change in the traditional Carolingian method of building churches with much thinner walls. One way of looking at the origins of Gothic architecture is to see it as a union of the Anglo-Norman method of using arches for the articulation of church interiors with a 'thin-wall' technique of construction. The essential feature of such a union would be that the arches could henceforth play a structural as well as a decorative role in the design. But in order to do so, they had to form themselves into a system—in fact, into a sort of skeleton—that could take the place of the great masses of the 'thick-wall' churches. When this happened, the walls would lose their structural primacy and assume a function rather like that of vault surfaces, namely that of enclosing space. In the skeleton of arches ribs performed an essential role, both as carrying members for whatever

superstructure was required, and visually as devices that conveyed a sense of connection and recession. Spaces covered by ribs (the French term '*croisée d'ogives*' is much more comprehensive than the English) became in effect identifiable compartments. And at this point architectural technicalities would begin to acquire iconographical significance. For if arches as such could define the spiritual ambiance of the Heavenly Jerusalem symbolically for two-dimensional images, the *croisée d'ogives* did so in a much more specified way for real or imitation people. In a sense, the original *croisée d'ogives* was the open ciborium over the altar and tomb of St Peter in the basilica at Rome. Long before the 12th century, that famous and venerable structure had been vaulted over; but we may be certain that something of its meaning had passed into the wider sphere of structural vaults, if only from the presence of something remarkably similar to it in the mosaic of the groined vault over the choir of S. Vitale at Ravenna. No doubt it is a long way from the 6th century to the 12th, and none of the surviving groined vaults over choirs belonging to the period have kept their original decoration. But there is nothing intrinsically improbable in the notion that the St Peter's idea was handed down as a convention for indicating that the particular space beneath was sacred. If this were so, then there is some justification for supposing that, for its own time as well as for the exponents of the Gothic Revival, Gothic as a style of architecture based on the *croisée d'ogives* was peculiarly suited for religious purposes.

It is not necessary to suppose that all the implications of Gothic architecture were at once apparent to the master of

St Denis. But a great many of them were. The delicacy of
the masonry in the new choir ran counter to the trend of
almost every great building in northern Europe of the previous half century. Instead of deep self-contained chapels,
the latter were more or less merged into an undulating
54,55 ripple on the exterior wall, while internally the removal of
all solid masonry allowed the windows that were their principal features to flood the whole choir with their coloured
light. Nothing of the superstructure has survived, but we
can infer from the incredibly slender dimensions of the
original columns that its elevation cannot have been very
great. Yet what there was must have been carried not on
the columns alone, but on the structural units of the compartments of the aisles and ambulatories. Most of these
61 features were to appear in the Ile de France cathedrals of
the next decade (the choir of St Denis was dedicated in
1144), and it is clear, whether or not we call St Denis itself
Gothic, that as a piece of architecture it stands more or less
at the head of a development which was to lead directly to
the Gothic cathedrals of the 13th century.

When we read the list of the prelates who attended the
consecration of St Denis, it is like a roll-call of churches
from the history books of architecture: Reims, Rouen, Sens,
Canterbury, Chartres, Soissons, Noyon, Orléans, Beau-
vais, Auxerre, Arras, Châlons, Coutances, Evreux, Thé-
rouanne, Meaux, Senlis. The only notable omissions from
the list are Cambrai, Laon, Amiens and Paris. With the
exception of Canterbury and the three from Normandy,
all of them came from the ecclesiastical provinces of Sens
and Reims; and although it would be wrong to think of the

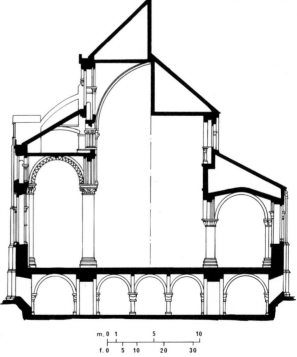

59. **Section through the choir of Canterbury cathedral.**
This section shows the rebuilt choir at Canterbury (plate 57)
in comparison with a reconstruction of the earlier building
burnt in 1174. Although the vault is supported by some of the
earliest examples of flying buttresses, which were eventually
to enable all the upper walls of a church to be of glass
(see figure 74) it also rests on thick walls, which
demonstrates how Anglo-Norman building techniques
continued into the early Gothic period.

respective bishops as returning home and straightaway setting about rebuilding their own cathedrals along the lines of what they had seen at St Denis, it is clear that they were in the habit of meeting together often and exchanging ideas about all manner of things, which no doubt included architecture. Their ecclesiastical connections reinforced the political links that bound them all to the affairs of the king of France. This was the basis on which the new style spread.

Although, to begin with, Gothic was very much a local style, the part of the world where it originated was already by the middle of the 12th century of more than local importance. To call this area the Ile de France is to connect it with the growing power and fortunes of the kingdom of France, and it is true that in the 13th century Gothic became an international style largely as a result of the prestige of France and her ruling dynasty. But in the 12th century these symptoms were not yet evident. It would be nearer the mark, perhaps, to describe the early Gothic zone as being on the French side of the old Mosan-Low Countries region, which ever since Carolingian times had been the real core of the political, cultural and industrial life of north-west Europe. In a sense the new style reflects a shift in the centre of gravity toward the west, and although the first manifestations were of a cultural order they cannot be explained wholly without reference to the upheavals of the so-called Investiture Contest. One of the permanent repercussions of that crisis was to break for ever the links which Carolingian, Ottonian and Salian Emperors had successively forged between their predominantly German states and the Church of Rome. But the successful effort which the Papacy made during the second half of the 11th century to emancipate itself from this particular instance of lay control only gave a new twist to the question as to what form relations between the Church and the world should take in the future. It very soon became apparent that the new international Papacy could not survive without some kind of secular support, and in practice, however long it was before the fact was overtly acknowledged, this support was sought from the western powers, England and France, but more especially from France. Throughout the 12th and 13th centuries a special relationship grew up between France and the Papacy, which culminated, if that is the right word, in the long succession of French popes and the 'Babylonian captivity' of the Papacy at Avignon in the 14th century. By that time, however, the international importance of the Church had dwindled and, deplorable as it must have seemed for the highest spiritual office in the world to be used as an asset in a game of power-politics, the degradation was of moral rather than practical significance.

67

60 (opposite). **The Liberal Arts.** South doorway on the west front of Chartres cathedral. Mid 12th century. The interests of the school of Chartres are shown by the appearance of the Liberal Arts on the voussoirs of this doorway, each personified by a woman, and represented by a classical philosopher. Note how these practically three-dimensional figures are fitted into the shape of the arch without the contortions found so often in earlier Romanesque sculpture.

61. **Nave of Laon cathedral,** looking west. Third quarter of the 12th century. The four-storeyed elevation, the sex-partite vault and the prolific use of slender monolithic columns and shafts are typical of this stage in the rapid development of the Gothic architecture of northern France. Compare the earlier cathedral of Tournai (figure 43) and the later ones of Chartres and Bourges (figure 73, plate 58).

In the 12th century things were different. Then the relationship was not so one-sided. In fact, if anything France stood to gain most. This was the period when northern France suddenly emerged as the centre of higher learning for the whole of Europe. What is known as the renaissance of the 12th century was an international phenomenon, and there was perhaps something indiscriminate about the voracious and seemingly insatiable way in which whatever there was to read, in whatever language, Greek, Arabic and Hebrew as well as Latin, and on whatever subject, was consumed at the behest of one of the most prodigious outbursts of curiosity the world has ever seen. It would be misleading to say that this movement was conducted by the Church for its own ends. Indeed, when the Church tried to control it, in the middle years of the 13th century, it was with the avowed purpose of preventing everything getting out of hand. But in the early stages, only churchmen had access to the literature that was available, and only they could read it. And before the dangers of heresy and paganism were fully realised, there was a widespread if somewhat touching assumption that everything that was written must in some way redound to the glory of God. So while the exuberant mood lasted, Church reform carried in its wake consequences of immense importance for European education. In the schools of northern France, and especially at Chartres, Reims, Laon and Paris, the traditional curriculum of the seven liberal arts came to be taught with a much enlarged reading list that included mathematicians like Euclid, as well as Plato and, later, Aristotle. If the Greek philosophers were ultimately responsible for provoking acute scholastic minds into the creation of the medieval science *par excellence*—theology—it is hardly claiming too much for Euclid to say that Gothic architecture was the child of 12th-century geometry.

60

While it is necessary to insist on the organic links between early Gothic architecture and its Romanesque antecedents, it is no less true that the style soon began to develop its own distinctive characteristics. One of the most pervasive of these was the amount of sheer geometry that was involved in a Gothic design. Take a cathedral like Laon which was started about 1160. Its interior presents to the beholder a multitude of columns, shafts and arches of varying size. In spite of the complexity, it can be shown that there is nothing haphazard about the distribution of its many components. The whole interior is composed around

61

a carefully worked out and surprisingly well integrated space frame, the mathematics of which were derived, knowingly or unknowingly, from the architectural traditions of classical antiquity. But quite apart from this, it is obvious to a cursory inspection that the arches and mouldings of such a building required stone cutting of a higher degree of precision than anything we find from the 11th century, and in the last resort all this was based on the application of geometry. Another way in which geometry was used was in the design of pointed arches. The days are long since passed when the presence of pointed arches could be regarded as one of the infallible signs that a building was Gothic. We have only to think of Cluny and Durham, two emphatically Romanesque buildings which nevertheless contained pointed arches, to realise the truth of this. But there is still a tendency to think of arches as either round or pointed, as though there were only two types. In fact, however, it is gradually becoming apparent that a great many arch forms were used in medieval architecture—elliptical, horseshoe, stilted, even perhaps something like catenary, as well as pointed and semicircular. And if in the end the pointed arch came into almost universal use, this was probably because it was the simplest and easiest to handle of all the arches whose height was not directly controlled by their span. Looked at in this way all the non-semicircular arches

57

62. **Villard d'Honnecourt.** *Page from a sketch-book* (MS. Fr. 19093, f. 17). 1230s. Bibliothèque Nationale, Paris. The use of pattern-books or sketch-books was widespread in the Middle Ages and of great importance in the diffusion of stylistic ideas. This figure is possibly derived from a mosaic at Monreale (figure 45) and analogies for the drapery style can be found at Reims, and in the work of Nicholas of Verdun.

63. **The Visitation.** *c.* 1220. Central porch on the west front of Reims cathedral. The overt classicism of this group, both in facial type and drapery style, suggests that the sculptor had knowledge of classical works. Compared with Chartres north transept (figure 52) these figures have, to a greater extent, broken away from the rigidity of earlier column figures.

go together, and it is possible to trace their history back beyond Gothic and Romanesque in western Europe to the architecture of Georgia, Byzantium and even the late Roman world of the eastern Mediterranean, where they connect up with a still more remote ancestry. But all this is by the way. What matters is that the pointed arches of Laon, and other Gothic churches as well, were constructed according to definite formulas, with the centres placed in preordained positions, and the radii of the arcs calculated in terms of the overall geometry of the design. In fact, the wholesale use of geometry came by the end of the 12th century to be perhaps the most characteristic feature of the mason's trade, the thing which marked him off from the virtuosi of the profession who produced what were in effect the cadenzas—the foliage capitals and perhaps even the stone figures of the portals.

GOTHIC VERSUS CLASSICAL

It may seem paradoxical to stress unduly the affinities, such as they are, between Gothic architecture and antiquity. If any style seems to embody all that distinguishes the Middle Ages from the classical world of Greece and Rome, it is surely Gothic. This was certainly how it seemed to the exponents of classical culture in Renaissance Italy. Brunelleschi could take the Romanesque Baptistery at Florence for an Early Christian or late antique building, but no one ever made the same mistake over a Gothic church. And even in the late Gothic north it was customary to convey the difference between the Old Testament and the New by using Romanesque forms to symbolise the former and Gothic the latter. Nevertheless, we must remember that unless there were watertight compartments of extraordinary efficiency early Gothic was, in some sense of the word, the architecture of the 12th-century renaissance and that, during precisely the same decades as it was developing in north-eastern France, the figure arts were undergoing a parallel transformation just to the east, but in a direction that was openly and frankly classical. This antinomy reaches a kind of climax at Reims in the early 13th century, where one of the most spectacular of the High Gothic cathedrals was provided with figure sculpture by one who, in default of his name, is significantly called 'the Master of the Antique Figures'. By 1220 it is unlikely that the sculp-

63, 88, 8

64. **Nicholas of Verdun.** *Jonah swallowed by the Whale.*
Detail of the Klosterneuburg altar. 1181. h. of centre
panel 5½ in. (14 cm.). Klosterneuburg, Austria.
65. **Three Kings shrine** (detail). *c.* 1200. Cathedral
Treasury, Cologne. This Jonah scene, believed to
prefigure the *Entombment of Christ* (compare plate 45), is one
of a series flanking scenes of New Testament events on the
altar (originally a pulpit) at Klosterneuburg, which is dated
1181 and signed by Nicholas of Verdun. On analogy with this,

and his other known work, a shrine at Tournai of 1205, part
of the Three Kings shrine at Cologne is also ascribed to him.
The relatively naturalistic figure style and distinctive drapery
with its mass of fine folds, found in both his enamelwork and
his cast figures, contrast strikingly with late Romanesque
traditions, and make Nicholas' work a precocious example of
a style which slightly later became popular in painting and
sculpture (plate 53, figures 52, 62, 63).

tor and master mason were the same man. But they must
have known one another well, and there can hardly have
been any serious disagreement between them as to the
limits beyond which it was improper to pursue classical
prototypes. Or even if there were, then we have in the
sketchbook of Villard de Honnecourt, who came from the
same milieu, indisputable indications that a classical
drapery style, if nothing else, was thought compatible with
Gothic architectural forms at that time. Up to a point,
therefore, there is good reason to think that when we encounter evidence of Gothic architects doing things in a
classical way they knew what they were doing, and we are
therefore entitled to ask why they stopped short. Why did
they not go further and produce buildings that really did
look classical, in the way that 12th-century churches like
Cluny and Autun, Pisa and Monreale, had tried to do. It
is of course true that all these buildings belonged, culturally
speaking, to the south, and that the enormous influence of

France, or more specifically northern France, during the
13th and 14th centuries (when it was every bit as overwhelming as in the time of Louis XIV) tended to act like
a brake on instinctive southern tendencies. But in sculpture,
in spite of the advantages of inheritance at the disposal of
12th-century Italians like Wiligelmo, Niccolò or Antelami,
it was the northerners, Nicholas of Verdun and the Master
of the Antique Figures at Reims, who were the first to grasp
what could be done with classical sculpture. No doubt
there were few classical buildings left in the north to serve
as models and, given the somewhat bizarre standards by
which the Middle Ages were prepared to recognise a copy
of something, it is just possible that architects really did
think they were building in the antique fashion when they
used antique proportions. But on the whole this is not likely.
It is far more probable that if they had wanted to make
Gothic classical they would have found ways of doing so
and that by refraining they had other ends in view.

66, **Albi cathedral.** Begun 1282. The fortress-like appearance of this vast cathedral, built in one of the former centres of the Albigensian heresy, has the austere simplicity typical of the southern French version of Gothic architecture. The fantastic elaboration of the late Gothic portal is a striking contrast.

67 (opposite). **Interior of La Chaise Dieu,** looking east. 1342–75. The establishment of the Popes at Avignon in the 14th century led to the creation of an important centre of artistic patronage in southern France. The abbey of La Chaise Dieu, built by Pope Clement VII, has, like Albi, a simple interior consisting of an aisleless nave with lateral chapels, a popular southern Gothic design.

This brings us face to face with what is, or ought to be, the central problem of Gothic, namely why there should have been such a style at all. In a very long-term view it is apt to seem decidedly odd that after all the tentative but impressive advances toward the recovery of classical techniques and styles, which, whatever qualifications and refinements we have recently seen fit to introduce, still provide our only justification for using a word like 'Romanesque', there should have been this long meander extending over some three hundred years before the next steps were taken toward the accomplishment of a genuine 'Renaissance'. If a brief answer has to be given, it can only be in terms of the attitude of the Church.

During the 13th century, that curious ambivalence in the Church's response to the legacy of the classical past, which ran like a thread from Tertullian in the 3rd century to the papal patrons of Michelangelo in the 16th, came to a head on numerous occasions. Generally speaking the Church has always been disposed to look favourably on classical scholarship in periods of tolerance, when the temperature of great issues was running low, and individuals could be safely allowed to do (more or less) what they liked. During the early Gothic period, however, the Church enjoyed, for the first and last time in its history, temporal power roughly commensurate with its own view of its own importance, and the responsibilities of power caused drastic reappraisals in many fields where laxity had hitherto prevailed. To use a somewhat unseemly metaphor, the Church behaved like a balloon, into which new ideas were constantly pumped. So long as there were few of these, they could be accommodated with little discomfort; but once the pressure was on, it became an open question whether the container could continue to expand, or whether it would burst. Up to a point the Church tried bravely to absorb the flood of strange thoughts that were dredged up

from the ancient books. Perhaps the most heroic of these efforts was that made by the theologians to square Aristotle with the doctrines of the Church, which occupied them for the greater part of the 13th century. But the spectacular condemnation in 1277 of 219 propositions taught at the university of Paris (mostly blamed on the infidel commentator Averroes, although they included a number held by St Thomas Aquinas himself) may be taken to mark the point at which this effort stopped. The momentous decision to call a halt to unfettered speculation at the highest or deepest level of medieval experience epitomises a predicament into which the Church gradually, and perhaps reluctantly, found itself forced at all levels. The situation was always in principle the same. There were aspects of ancient life and thought that were beyond question wrong if what the Church taught was right. Limits, therefore, had to be drawn somewhere. The idea of paganism was intimately connected with the idea of heresy. In this respect, long before the rarefied intellectual wrangle at Paris, a far more dangerous crisis had arisen in the south-west of France, where there had come to flourish an entire way of life that was inconsistent with the precepts of the Church. By 1200 this scandal could no longer be ignored. It had to be either condoned or proscribed. The bloody glee with which the proscription was executed, in what is known as the Albigensian Crusade during the first decades of the 13th century, already betrays the mood of the Inquisition, which was established shortly afterwards to prevent the same kind of thing happening again elsewhere.

The fundamental sin of the Albigeois, even if it was not mentioned, was their tendency to regard the orthodox Catholic priesthood as superfluous. This was, of course, to cut at the very root of the Church's grip on the secular world, and it is conceivable that, if the rather precocious civilisation which flourished at the higher levels of this

66

heretical society had been allowed to grow unhindered, it might eventually have reached a secular position and point of view similar to that of the 14th-century Italian humanists. As it was, however, the whole of the western Mediterranean coastlands were affected by the zealotry which followed the Albigensian Crusade, and any Renaissance symptoms there were set back by at least two hundred years.

CHURCH VERSUS STATE

But of all the enemies who threatened danger to the Church's position, it was perhaps inevitable after the Investiture Contest that the one to evoke the most acute apprehension should have been the medieval Empire. Although in the end it was the national governments that grew out of the feudal monarchies of western Europe which reduced the Papacy to a level of resounding impotence, all the arguments and propaganda of the great debates of the 11th and 12th centuries saw the Emperor as the Pope's natural antagonist. Each inherited the same theory of government, the only difference being the identity of the keystone that should crown the whole edifice of human society, under God. In the nature of the case no compromise was possible, and in practice solutions were only reached by the surrender, tacit or otherwise, of important claims by one or other of the contenders. Ultimately the whole of the Church's attitude toward classical art and architecture turned on the degree to which these were contaminated by their inevitable association with the very idea of the Empire.

It was the essence of the papal case that the Pope was placed 'as mediator between God and man—less than God, but more than man,' as Innocent III put it. In Imperial language he was indeed more truly emperor than the Emperor, and from this point of view there was some jus-

tification for the Church taking over all the trappings of Empire, including Imperial art. Ideas such as these seem to have lain behind the numerous classical allusions at Cluny, though they were carefully mixed with others derived from Early Christian sources. On the whole, however, the Church preferred to think of itself as something beyond and above the Empire, and in so far as it pondered seriously on the implications of its patronage of art and architecture the advantages of having so to speak its own style, free from all embarrassing associations with the other side, must have seemed overwhelming. But in any case too much classicism, and especially overt classicism, was undesirable in a Christian Church. It was yet another case of a line having to be drawn in the interests of ecclesiastical prudence. As the feud between successive Popes and the Hohenstaufen Emperor Frederick II moved toward its hysterical and unedifying climax in the middle years of the 13th century, the position of the Church in this matter must have seemed by implication to have shifted still further, to one of uncompromising hostility. Although the Emperor did not exactly preach anti-sacerdotalism, he appears to have practised it on a sufficiently repugnant scale to make himself the focus of all the heresies, and these, added to the sins of his office and his person, qualified him in the eyes of the Church for the unenviable role of Antichrist. So long as the animosities that were generated in this quarrel lasted, a lingering stigma seems to have attached itself to the study of classical art. Even when the literary Renaissance had begun, one of the most interesting things about it from a medieval point of view was the extraordinary lapse of time before artists followed suit, and genuine antiquities were copied in an uninhibited way; and another was the tenacity of Gothic traditions, even in the heart of Italy. In fact, the whole Gothic episode, so far as the south was concerned, stemmed in large measure from the Church's dread of

96

98

heresy, whether in its Albigensian or Hohenstaufen forms. Gothic was never truly at home in the Mediterranean world, and its presence there calls for something more by way of explanation than the pseudo-biological operations of the spirit of the times. Historically the answer is that it was there because the Church wanted it to be there. In short, Gothic was in a sense the Church's own style. Precisely because it was an interloper in the south, this conclusion may be grasped more readily there than in the north, where Gothic was at home.

Just when the Church decided to adopt Gothic, or indeed, whether any conscious decision along these lines was ever taken at all, is uncertain. But if we have to pick any single event as marking the point where Gothic ceased to be the local style of north-eastern France and the regions round about, including parts of England, and became an international style (the first of its kind) this would have to be the fourth Lateran Council of 1215, which marked the climax of the pontificate of Innocent III. Innocent's reign (1198–1216) has always been taken as the high-water mark in the fortunes of the medieval Papacy. During those years the Church approached more closely than at any other time in its history to the reformers' ideal of a totally emancipated, supranational organisation, with the Pope himself recognised by most, if not all, of the secular rulers of Christendom as their feudal overlord. To the prelates who met together at Rome in 1215 the occasion must have seemed one that justified a great deal of exultation, and if there was any discussion of church architecture it is likely to have been in terms of victory monuments.

Whatever may have happened at the fourth Lateran Council, in the years which followed the diffusion of Gothic began to assume the form of something like a systematic campaign. Gothic had already reached England in 1174, when the choir of Canterbury was rebuilt after a fire. Here its presence is to be explained by the close connections that prevailed all through the 12th century between Canterbury and the ecclesiastical polity of northern France. In Spain something that perhaps deserves to be called Gothic is to be found in the cathedral of Cuenca (after 1183), where there are decided connections with the proto-Gothic of Burgundy. But generally, where symptoms of Gothic occur elsewhere in these two countries at the end of the 12th century, it is due directly or indirectly to the enterprise of the local Cistercians. St Bernard's order was not actively committed to the promotion of Gothic as a style, but the austerity of its simpler forms provided a useful foil to the more exuberant kinds of Romanesque, which were particularly prevalent in the western extremities of Europe. It is significant that in Germany and Italy in the 12th century the part played by the Cistercians in introducing Gothic was far less conspicuous. There the native forms of Romanesque were usually innocuous enough to require no active measures to escape their insidious influence.

The spread of Gothic in the early 13th century was conducted in different ways at different levels. At the top, so to speak, where dynastic or ecclesiastical prestige was involved, and only the best would do, we find more or less straight imports from France. This is what happened at Burgos (1222) and Toledo (1227) in Spain. The English, already having their own kind of Gothic, and therefore not needing to import anyone else's, proceeded on their own insular way. During the first half of the 13th century England was perhaps more isolated from the continent than at any other time since the Norman Conquest, and it is therefore not surprising that the Gothic which evolved there should have been, to say the least, eccentric. Some of the eccentricities, however, particularly the asymmetrical vaults of Lincoln, were to suggest possibilities of waywardness that were eagerly followed up by late Gothic Germans (but not until the 14th century). The Germans themselves were much more cautious. At Maulbronn and Ebrach the Cistercians at last gave some sort of belated lead, but it was not really until Cologne was started in 1248, and the nave of Strasbourg two years later, that they plunged wholeheartedly into the task of mastering the new style. Nothing is more remarkable than the difference between the German response on the one hand to Gothic architecture and on the other to Gothic sculpture. The possibilities of the latter they seem to have grasped instinctively. The former they had to learn, slowly and even laboriously. In fairness, however, it must be admitted that when they had passed through their long apprenticeship they emerged as masters equal to the French. And thanks to historical circumstances over which they had no control, the Germans had far more opportunity to display their talents during the later Middle Ages than did the French, with the result that the period 1350–1500 is apt to appear in the history books of medieval art as an age dominated by the Germans.

In the south of Europe, that is from Aragón to Italy, the overwhelming impression is that Gothic was imposed from above, that it was accepted reluctantly and grasped only superficially. To a very considerable extent it was promoted by the new orders of friars, Innocent III's special international agencies for ensuring the 'togetherness' of Church and people. This meant that right from the start there was a tendency for Gothic churches to be bare and barn-like and, apart from one or two easily identifiable intruders among the later cathedrals in the area, southern Gothic retained this character. The consequences of this were deceptively far-reaching, as we shall see in due course. Just how perfunctory the southern response to Gothic could be is apparent in out of the way churches like the Cistercian S. Nicola at Agrigento in Sicily, where there are pointed arches and ribbed vaults, but nothing else to remind a northern Frenchman of home.

It may seem perverse to consider these peripheral forms of Gothic before the central masterpieces. But it is as well to be reminded of the tremendous difference in performance between the home product and the foreign copy. In a comparatively small area of northern France, and over a period of perhaps no more than one man's lifetime,

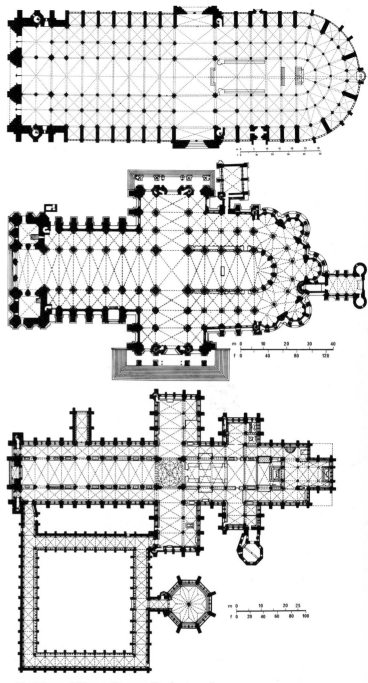

59, 61,
73
a series of cathedrals were built that successively perfected an image worthy of the arrogance, the power and the sublimity of Pope Innocent's conception of the Catholic Church. If he bestowed the favour of his approval on the style of these monuments, his instinct was unerring. And even if he did not, the higher clergy of the Church drew the the appropriate conclusion for themselves.

CHARTRES

69
From a French Gothic point of view, the fifty years between 1190 and 1240 were the most auspicious of the whole Middle Ages. At Chartres (1194) and at Bourges (before 1195) in France, two great designs were worked out, which in their respective ways utterly transformed the whole scale of church building in that country. It was not just a question of enlarging the size of existing members. On the contrary both involved the radical rethinking of accepted formulas, and both achieved spectacular effects that had not been seen before in the West. At Chartres everything was sacrificed to the presentation of two vast iconographical programmes—of sculpture in the portals, and of glass in the windows. The architect of Chartres must have been one of the most self-effacing men of genius ever to have graced his profession. It was his task to prepare a frame-
73
work in which other men's talents would be displayed; and the fact that it is still the statues and the windows that people go to see at Chartres is a back-handed token of his success. One is apt to forget the liberties that he took and the risks he ran by attempting the unprecedented. For the sake of the windows he removed the traditional galleries of 12th-century cathedrals, he enlarged the arcades and he heightened the clearstorey. Above all, to secure the fragile box of glass that reared itself far above the roofs of the aisles, he resorted to the relatively new device of flying buttresses, which he piled up around the church like a permanent scaffolding of stone. Compared with the brilliance of colour
35
in the windows and the narrative interest of their subject-matter, there is little in the actual stonework to catch one's eye. And it is the same outside. No one pauses for long to
52
examine the buttresses when the portals are to be admired. This architecture is just superb structural engineering.

As an image of the Church Triumphant, Chartres is perhaps the most ambitious (and providentially still complete) thing of its kind. Nowhere else are the great themes of Christian doctrine and the Christian view of history presented in such a universal and, at the same time, such a particular way. It is the building that above all others seems to convey the mood of the Lateran gathering. From this point of view, we may perhaps be allowed to single out for special mention the confrontation across the central doorway of the north transept of *St Peter*, decked out in the
52
splendid robes of a 13th-century Pope, and *Melchizedek*, the priest-king of the Old Testament, who was here, typologically, St Peter's forerunner. It was an identification much favoured by Pope Innocent, and the images at Chartres must surely have been intended to refer to him.

68. **Plan of Notre Dame, Paris.** *c.* 1163.
69. **Plan of Chartres cathedral.** 1194.
70. **Plan of Salisbury cathedral.** 1220. Notre Dame, whose choir was consecrated in 1163, has one of the simplest cathedral plans devised during the experimental period of the 12th century in northern France. The absence of projecting transepts or chapels must be explained by the desires of the architects, rather than by liturgical needs; it was found necessary to add chapels soon afterwards. Compared with the simplicity of Notre Dame, Chartres goes to the opposite extreme with a very prominent transept and an uneven ring of chapels, the plan of the latter partly conditioned by the chapels of the 11th-century crypt beneath. This type of east end, though usually with regular chapels, became standard in French High Gothic churches. English 13th-century cathedrals such as Salisbury generally did not adopt the French *chevet*, but preferred square east ends with parallel projecting chapels. The double transept was also a popular feature. Instead of the great western portals of French cathedrals, the English preferred lateral porches.

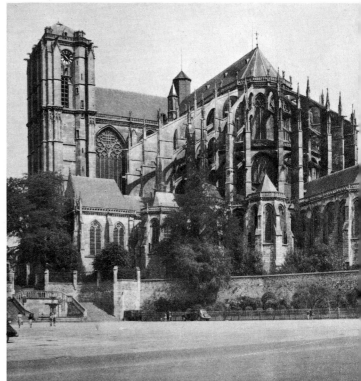

74 (above). **East end of Le Mans cathedral.** Begun 1218. Note the immense height of the clearstorey of this building, whose vaults are supported by a complex series of flying buttresses. Compare the transparency of this Gothic *chevet* with the solid masses of a Romanesque east end such as Conques (figure 32).

71 (opposite, left). **Vault of St Hugh's choir, Lincoln cathedral.** Begun 1192. The new Gothic works at Lincoln incorporated many ideas from the slightly earlier choir at Canterbury; this vault, however, is a new departure. English Gothic took up the ridge rib, and the principle of multiple ribs diverging from a single point, but not the asymmetry of this arrangement, which remains unique.

72 (opposite, right). **North transept rose window** of Notre Dame, Paris. Mid-13th century. In the 13th century the clearstorey of Notre Dame was heightened and rose windows added to the transepts, to bring this early Gothic cathedral into line with the latest ideas of 'Rayonnant' architecture—the name derives from the centrifugal radiating tracery patterns found in rose windows such as this.

73 (opposite, below left). **Nave of Chartres cathedral.** 1194. The elevation of Chartres, with its tall arcade, narrow triforium and immense clearstorey (compare Laon, figure 61) became the standard type for the French High Gothic cathedral. At Chartres the windows are still either lancets, or openings grouped together as in the clearstorey to form 'plate tracery'. Compare the more delicate effect of bar tracery, invented slightly later (figure 77).

BOURGES AND LE MANS

Bourges is a more complex building than Chartres, and conversely, although there is some magnificent glass and some interesting sculpture there, it is the architecture that commands our deepest attention. There is no transept at Bourges and, perhaps because of the spatial unity that this ensures, it is the one great vaulted hall of its kind that invites comparison across the centuries with those of Imperial Rome. Certainly the arrangement of its nave and four aisles in echelon calls to mind one of the most distinctive features of old St Peter's and S. Paolo fuori le Mura in Rome, or for that matter Romanesque Cluny which was itself inspired from that quarter. In its own more subtle way, this allusion conveys much the same meaning as the *St Peter* and *Melchizedek* at Chartres. We are invited to think of Bourges as a reiteration in the Church's new style of its venerable Early Christian archetypes. But in other ways Bourges broke new ground. Like Chartres, it also has no gallery, only here all the gain has been concentrated in the arcades, with the result that these are quite prodigious.. Moreover, the columns on which they are carried do not stop short at their capitals. Instead, they seem to push on upwards through the walls until they meet the ribs of the vaults. The effect of this is to make the residual bits of wall above the arcades seem no more than screens, stretched from one pillar to the next. There are no structural reasons why they should not be dispensed with. And in the choir of Le Mans (started 1218), which was one of the progeny of Bourges, this next logical step was taken. The impression at Le Mans is quite staggering. A huge arcade is surmounted by nothing more substantial than a row of great clearstorey win-

dows. There is hardly any masonry to be seen in the entire elevation, and in spite of its great size the whole design has the kind of delicacy that would be more appropriate in a reliquary casket. It is small wonder that, outside, this reliquary of masonry is clasped by the most extensive array of flying buttresses in the whole of France. Whatever one thinks of the masonry at Chartres, here structure reaches the level of the most consummate art.

REIMS

One of the more amazing things about the Gothic cathedrals of northern France that were built in the fifty years or so after Chartres and Bourges is the way in which each of them contrived to preserve its own individuality. No two are alike, even though they were all devoted to a single end and shared a common repertory of skills and experience. At Reims (started 1211), apart from the sculpture to which we shall return, the great innovation was bar tracery. This began as a device for breaking up the growing apertures of lancet windows by inserting thin patterns of cut stone into what were in effect holes too large for the ordinary lead and iron armatures that held the glass. Very soon, however, the link between tracery and windows ceased to be exclusive, and it became a kind of abstract ornament that could be applied almost universally—to walls, over voids or simply left free-standing.

The implications for the future of this new development at Reims were to prove almost incalculable. If any single invention permits us to distinguish earlier from later Gothic architecture, this was it. It is hardly a coincidence that the anonymity which shrouds the great structural engineers of the Chartres-Bourges era should suddenly have dispersed when we turn to Reims. We know the names of all the master-masons who worked at Reims, and the same is true of Amiens, Westminster and Cologne. It is as though masons suddenly acquired a new kind of reputation that made them memorable and, while this may have had something to do with wider changes in the social habits of the 13th century, it also surely reflects a change in the professional status of the masons themselves.

Essentially tracery was a kind of ornament, and it was a kind of ornament that the masons themselves could produce. In the process of specialisation which went on all through the 12th century, anyone with an outstanding talent for cutting stone tended to be channelled into the field of pure sculpture. This consisted of giving relief to two-dimensional drawings and, as we have seen, the sculptors tended either to get these directly from metalworkers or manuscript illuminators, or else they learnt how to make them for themselves from the same sources as the metalworkers and manuscript illuminators. The result of this was that a man of genius like the designer of Chartres had hardly anything to do with the decoration of his cathedral. With the invention of tracery, however, the masons began to make a spectacular come-back. Whether or not the decline in the sheer amount of sculpture that we find

75. **Charlemagne shrine.** Early 13th century. Silver-gilt, copper-gilt, enamel, filigree, precious stones. 80¼ × 37 × 22½ in. (204 × 94 × 57 cm.). Cathedral Treasury, Aachen. Although architectural detail is used on this shrine—the ends are gabled, and the figures set under arcades— it has a far more tomb-like appearance than do the later Gothic shrines. The reliefs on the cover show scenes from the life of Charlemagne (see plate 46).

76. **Shrine of St Gertrude** (detail). After 1272. 70¾ × 21¼ × 31½ in. (180 × 54 × 80 cm.). Formerly in the convent church of St Gertrude, Nivelles (destroyed 1940). Compared with the Charlemagne shrine (figure 75) this reliquary with its rose windows, pinnacles and niches is nothing less than a church in miniature. Although, paradoxically, it still has reliefs on the roof, it looks forward to the architectural fantasies of such 14th-century reliquaries as the Three Towers shrine at Aachen (plate 66).

in later Gothic cathedrals is to be explained in this way (tracery was much cheaper than sculpture), there is little doubt that tracery was one of the factors involved in the fundamental change that took place in the painting of stained glass during the second half of the 13th century. **35, 59 60, 61** Instead of the deep-toned glass that we find at Chartres or Bourges, this became perceptibly lighter, and instead of being fired into the glass much of the colour was simply painted on the surface. In both these ways stained glass became a far more delicate art, less like enamelling, and much more like translucent painting. And in the process the tracery in which it was set itself became far more visible.

But the repercussions extended further. Like space frames, arches and mouldings, tracery designs were basically a question of applied geometry. But a new factor now entered the situation. This was what might be called architectural drawing. No doubt there had been drawing of a kind from the time ashlar had to be cut to precise profiles. What was special about Gothic tracery drawing was its often extreme elaboration, which called for an order **72** of skill with rulers and compasses quite unknown before, and the fact that to be useful at all it had to be done to scale. This idea of scale is of crucial importance. It at once establishes the possibility of kinship between very large and very small forms; and from this there opens up the prospect of an entire field of application for the new kind of drawing, outside the limits of architecture properly so-called. This is precisely what happened. Apropos of Romanesque drawing, it was suggested that its firm lines betrayed the dominant influence of metalwork. In the 13th century the whole question of dependence and interrelation among the arts was given a fresh twist by the arrival on the scene of this new kind of drawing. First and foremost we can see its effect on metalwork itself. If we compare one of the late Romanesque **43, 7** reliquaries, like that of St Elizabeth at Marburg in Germany (c. 1236), with, first, the shrine of St Taurin at **65** Evreux in France (c. 1250) and then that of St Gertrude at **76** Nivelles in Belgium (after 1272), the process of transformation unfolds before our eyes. The first, in spite of its 'transepts' and gables, is still basically conceived as a sarcophagus. The last is, to all intents and purposes, a miniature Gothic church. But if shrines became churches, churches also became shrines, and in the formal equation of church and reliquary, already foreshadowed in Romanesque times, we have a clue to most, and the best, of the monumental and decorative art in northern Europe between 1250 and the Reformation.

(Continued on page 129)

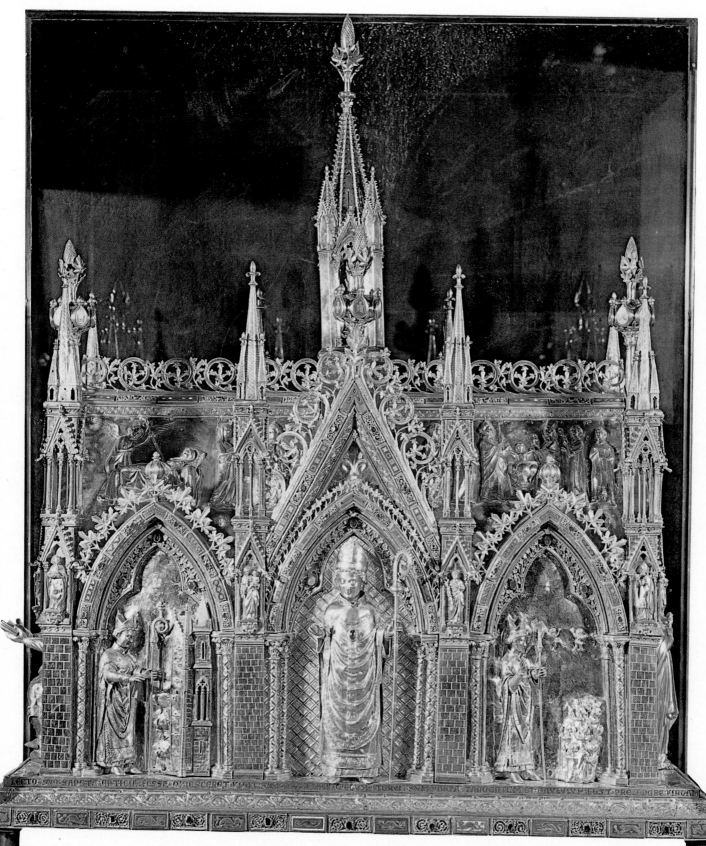

65. **Shrine of St Taurin.** 1240–53. Silver and gilded copper with enamel plaques. h. 28 in. (70 cm.). Church of St Taurin, Evreux, Normandy. This reliquary illustrates the crucial transition in the design of this class of object that occurred in the middle of the 13th century, i.e. from something basically conceived as a tomb to something modelled on a church or chapel. Hence the significance of the architectural detail.

66 (opposite). **Three Towers reliquary.**
c. 1370. Silver gilt with enamel plaques.
37 × 29 in. (94 × 74 cm.). Cathedral
Treasury, Aachen. The insubstantial
beauty of this reliquary, when compared
with the shrine of St Taurin at Evreux
(plate 65) or the Shrine of St Gertrude,
Nivelles (figure 76), shows on a small scale
how far architectural concepts had moved
from the more solid forms of the 13th
century. Far more care is lavished on the
framework than on the figures themselves.

67 (right). **Detail of the niche-work in
the Lady Chapel, Ely cathedral.**
c. 1310. The niche-work of Ely Lady
Chapel is among the most refined
examples of small-scale, decorative
carving of the English Decorated period
(*c.* 1250–1350). The arches are
characterised by what are called 'nodding
ogees', i.e. they not only undulate but are
broken forward to form canopies.

68. **Detail from the choir stalls,
Chester cathedral.** *c.* 1380. Wood. The
intricate carving of these choir stalls is
typical of the late medieval obsession with
elaborate architectural decoration. It can
be compared not only with such small-
scale objects as the Three Towers shrine
(plate 66), but also with the great
cathedral spires (see figure 85).

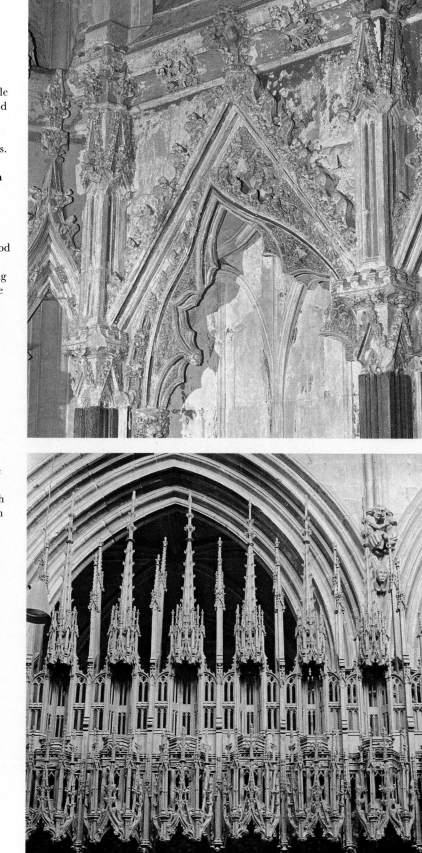

69. **Silver altar** (detail). Begun 1287,
completed *c*. 1396. Overall height over
7 ft. (215 cm.). Cathedral, Pistoia. The
fact that the current European
preoccupation with niche-work extended
also to Italy can be seen in this altar, which,
although ordered in 1287 to house a relic
of St James the Great, was much added to
in the 14th century. The figure of Christ
shown here dates from about 1353 and is
the work of Giulio Pisano. The smaller
figures are earlier.

70. **The Sufferings of Job.** Jamb sculpture on the Virgin Porch, Notre Dame, Paris. *c.* 1220. This is an example on a small scale from the 'classical' period of early Gothic sculpture. Compare the style of this naturalistic group of figures with the monumental column figures of Reims and Chartres (figures 52, 63).

71. **The Bamberg Rider.** *c.* 1236. Nearly life-size. Bamberg cathedral. The statue was probably intended to stand over a doorway. The identity of the Rider has never been established. Various kings of Germany associated with Bamberg have been suggested, including Frederick II. Whoever he is, the Rider embodies contemporary German ideals of knightly virtue.

72 (above). **Master of Naumburg.** *The Last Supper*. After 1249. h. *c.* 36 in. (91 cm.). West choir screen, Naumburg cathedral. One of the scenes of the Passion. Observe the great attention given to purely ephemeral gestures. All six figures are doing something that would be different a moment later or a moment before. It is this that makes the Naumburg screen one of the dramatic masterpieces of Gothic sculpture.

73 (left). **Master of Naumburg.** *Ekkehard and Uta*. After 1249. Life-size. West choir, Naumburg cathedral. One of the pair of figures representing the founders of the cathedral and their wives. Ekkehard was Margrave of Meissen (1032–46). Uta was a Polish princess. As retrospective portraits they may be modelled on 13th-century contemporaries.

74 (opposite). **Gabelcrucifix, or Pestkreuz.** 1304. Wood. Over life-size. Church of St Maria im Kapitol, Cologne. In this extraordinarily horrid statue of Christ on the Cross, his sufferings have been deliberately exaggerated, and his body distorted to make it into a caricature, designed to evoke both terror and pity. This was to become a characteristic feature of one strand of later Gothic art in Germany.

75 (opposite). **Giovanni Pisano.** *Pulpit.* Completed 1301. S. Andrea, Pistoia. The inscription on the pulpit praises Giovanni as being 'blessed with higher skill' than his father Nicola Pisano, and the emotionalism which fills his figures, with their swaying Gothic forms, is the antithesis of Nicola's monumental classicism (compare figures 96, 98).

76 (right). **Virgin and Child.** 1339. Silver gilt. h. 27¼ in. (69 cm.). Louvre, Paris. This figure of the Virgin, presented by Jeanne d'Evreux, wife of Charles le Bel of France, to the abbey of St Denis reflects the increasing sophistication demanded by royal patrons. The rich effect of the statuette is enhanced by the enamelled scenes from the life of Christ round the base.

77. **Virgin and Child.** First half of the 14th century. Notre Dame, Paris. The composition of the *Virgin and Child*, very popular in Gothic art, was repeated so often that inevitably many of the works appear stereotyped. This *Virgin* from Notre Dame, when compared with the silver *Virgin* of Jeanne d'Evreux (plate 76), seems, in spite of her elegance, stiff and unoriginal.

78 (opposite). **A page from the Maciejowski Old Testament** (MS. 638 f. 3r). *c.* 1250. 15⅜ × 11¾ in. (39 × 30 cm.). This manuscript, illuminated in Paris, was presented to Shah Abbas the Great of Persia by a papal mission in 1608, and at his request the Latin descriptions were translated into Persian. The extremely lively scenes illustrate episodes in the Old Testament, from the Creation to the life of David. The ones on this page show *The Drunkenness of Noah*, *The Building of the Tower of Babel*, *The Sacrifice of Isaac*, and *The Leading of the Children of Israel into Captivity*.

...valiter Noe uineam plantauit. et mox
ebrius ac nudatus. ab uno filiorum ir...
a duobus uerecunde contegitur.

...alii muro regionis erigit. et mox et alto
prospiciens lingua humana consundit lingua. ne se inuicem hedificantes intelligant.
Atqui ita ceptum opus non possit impleri.

Qualiter Abraam iubente deo filium. a obe-
diens sacrificare filium suum unicum no-
lens iam eleuato gladio ut feriret. ab angelo
retrahitur. et aries pter spem oblatus sacrifi-
cio destinatur.

Quomodo excitus Regis Elamitarum cali-
orum trium regum. Victo rege gomorre et
aliis quatuor regibus. captiuos ducunt. zinc
aliis Loth nepotem habeale.

79. **St Peter.** Detail from the Westminster Retable. Late 13th century. Westminster abbey. This retable, though much damaged, is one of the finest examples of English painting at this date, combining an Italianate modelling of the draperies with the slender elegance of the French and English court styles. There is no attempt, however, to create an illusion of space, and the background is conventional diaperwork.

80. **The Crucifixion.** From the Psalter of Robert de Lisle (MS. Arundel 83 part II, f. 132r). Before 1339. 13¾ × 9 in. (35 × 23 cm.). British Museum, London. The East Anglian school of illumination, to which this manuscript belongs, is remarkable for its riotous border decoration, but this page shows a dignity and restraint more usually associated with large-scale painting. The plastic modelling of the draperies adds depth to a composition in which even the architectural motifs are merely part of the overall decorative design.

81 (opposite). **Jean Pucelle.** *The Annunciation.* From the Book of Hours of Jeanne de Savoie (f. 13r). Second quarter of the 14th century. 7 × 5 in. (18 × 13 cm.). Musée Jacquemart-André, Paris. The influence of Jean Pucelle was such that motifs from his works are still to be found in books produced some fifty years after his death. His elegant, swaying

figures and charming marginal grotesques became, in the hands of his workshop, somewhat stereotyped, but his first-hand knowledge of Italian painting gave a new impulse to French illumination.

82 (above). **Master Consolus.** *A Miracle of St Benedict.* Second half of the 13th century. Fresco. Lower church,

monastery of Sacro Speco, Subiaco. The solid stocky figures of this fresco provide a sharp contrast to the attenuated forms beloved of northern Gothic artists (see plates 79 and 80). The rocky cave in which the saint sits gives a three-dimensional quality to the painting, although the little trees are a conventional stylisation.

83. **The Betrayal of Christ** (detail). Third quarter of the 14th century. Wall-painting. Lower church, monastery of Sacro Speco, Subiaco. This detail from the Passion shows the apostles fleeing from the scene of the betrayal of Christ. Although Sienese origins are traceable in the facial types, the heavy figures have none of the refinement of the Sienese school (see plate 87).

77. **Nave of the abbey church of
St Denis.** Second quarter of the 13th
century. Suger's works at the east and
west ends of St Denis (see figures 54, 55)
are now linked by a 13th-century
'Rayonnant' nave and transepts. Wall
surfaces are reduced to a minimum by
the enormous expanse of the bar
tracery clearstorey windows, and even
the outer wall of the triforium is glazed
(compare plates 60, 61).

THE SAINTE CHAPELLE

Unquestionably the finest and most celebrated of all the church-reliquaries was the Sainte Chapelle in Paris. This was built in the royal palace to house a fragment of the Crown of Thorns, which was bought by Louis IX (St Louis) from the impecunious Latin Emperor at Constantinople in 1239. The relic arrived in 1241, and the chapel was ready by 1248. It consisted of upper and lower chambers, reminiscent of the palace chapel at Aachen. But the upper chapel is what really matters. It is a veritable glass-house, and in fact resembles in so many details the cathedral of Amiens that we are entitled to regard it as the work of someone from that town, where the choir was at that very moment in the course of construction. There is, therefore, some specific ground for thinking of the chapel as the clearstorey of a cathedral choir, transposed and set up as a free-standing structure. But the converse is also true. We are entitled to conclude that the upper parts of a cathedral choir were themselves conceived as a kind of chapel destined to contain a reliquary. This has already been suggested in the case of Le Mans, but it is perhaps even more obvious at Amiens and Cologne. External and, better still, aerial views of these cathedrals from the east, bring out with great clarity an abrupt change of style between the relatively austere chapels of the lower half of the building and the clearstorey of the upper, in which all the decorative enrichments are concentrated. It is known that when Cologne cathedral was rebuilt in 1248, the explicit purpose was to provide a more worthy setting for Nicholas of Verdun's shrine of the Three Kings, and the fact that Amiens was selected as its principal model closes a neat ring of connections between these three buildings. Together they provide the two basic prototypes for the smart churches of the future—the reliquary chapel, and a new, tracery-decorated version of the High Gothic cathedral. The style they have in common is usually called Rayonnant.

Although Rayonnant developed naturally out of the invention of tracery and although in many respects it was no more than a refinement of what had been achieved in the High Gothic cathedrals, nevertheless it coincided with one of the great divides in medieval history. Precise lines of demarcation are deceptive and difficult to draw here. But it is true to say that after the middle of the 13th century there are symptoms of a pervading mood of disillusionment, and that by the end of the century the high hopes and self-confidence which had sustained the buoyancy of the previous two hundred years had all but evaporated. The generation that grew to manhood in Europe after the death

78. **Choir of Gloucester cathedral,** looking east. *c.* 1337.
In the 14th century the Romanesque arcades and galleries
of Gloucester choir were concealed by a screen of tracery, and
a vast window was inserted in the east wall. The
Perpendicular style, of which this is one of the earliest
examples, derives its name from the predominating vertical
tracery bars—a radical change from the flowing curves of
Decorated tracery (figures 79, 80).

79. **Window in the Octagon of Ely cathedral.** 1322–42.
80 (opposite, left). **Nave windows of Exeter cathedral.**
Mid-14th century. The windows in the elaborate octagonal
crossing of Ely, which replaced the Norman tower after its
collapse in 1322, have the flowing tracery typical of English

of St Louis (1270) subscribed to few of the ideals which
had dazzled their grandparents or even their parents. With
the fall of Acre in 1291 the Crusade was virtually acknowledged to be a lost cause. The pretensions if not the myth of
the medieval Empire had been destroyed by the Papacy in
its fight to the death with the Hohenstaufen, and in con-
triving to survive, the Papacy itself had pawned away its
spiritual prestige. After the humiliation of Boniface VIII
at Anagni in 1303, no one, not even the Popes themselves,
took seriously their claim to exercise the complete authority. Even the heroic effort of St Thomas to demonstrate
that the operations of the rational intellect were entirely
compatible with the dogmas of the Christian faith seems to
have convinced his immediate successors far less than remote posterity. An age of exuberance slowly dissolved into
one of scepticism and retrenchment, and with the extinc-
tion of familiar terms of reference there was inevitably a
certain amount of confusion as to the right way to turn
next. By and large the instinct of the 14th century was to
demand new sources of authority less fallible than reason or
tradition. These were sought in many directions—in the
Bible itself, in the unquestionable immediacy of mystical
experience, in the *de facto* power of secular governments
and, not least, by a few poets and scholars in Italy, from
the records of the accomplishments of classical antiquity.

So far as patronage was concerned, the main long-term
effect of these changes was that the laity took the place of
the Church as its principal source. The lead here was taken
by the French royal family. That most Christian king, St
Louis, made it his business to serve the Faith in ways that he

considered appropriate to his station, that is by lavishing
on holy relics the expensive luxuries that he denied himself
and his court. Other members of his family did likewise,
though their motives became progressively less unworldly.
Rayonnant was very much the French court style. The
name is derived from the characteristic tracery pattern of 72
the rose windows that are frequently found in French
churches from about 1240 onwards, and these, wherever
they occur, are sure pointers to the influence of Paris. As 60, 77
the king's power spread more and more effectively across
the length and breadth of France, so we can trace Rayonnant architecture following in its wake—into Normandy,
the Loire valley, the south and the south-west. Imperceptibly from being a royal style it became a national, and
even an international, style. If it was the Church's policy
to promote the advance of Gothic to the limits of Christendom, this wish was fulfilled in the 14th century, though
perhaps not in the way that Pope Innocent had desired.
For it was on the prestige of France rather than of the
Church that Rayonnant was carried across the Channel to
England, across the Pyrenees to Spain and across the Rhine 60
into Germany.

GOTHIC IN ENGLAND

The fortunes of Rayonnant Gothic in England were very
much at the mercy of entrenched insular prejudices. In a
sense the whole architectural history of England between
1250 and 1350 can be seen as a running battle between
protagonists of the alien style, whose headquarters was the
court in London, and the guardians of the native tradition,

architecture of the Decorated period, particularly in northern England. The nave windows of Exeter illustrate the diversity of intricate tracery patterns found in this style, which continued side by side in the 14th century with the new Perpendicular tracery (see figure 78).

81. **West façade of Rouen cathedral.** First half of the 15th century. Although the tracery patterns found on the elaborate Gothic façade of Rouen cathedral can be compared with those developed earlier in England (figures 79, 80) the use of transparent screenwork to cover a whole façade is typical of French Flamboyant architecture.

whose strength was mainly in the west country. Not one of the great royal buildings of this period, Westminster abbey (1245), St Stephen's chapel in the palace of Westminster (1290), or the choir of what is now the cathedral of Gloucester (1336), can be truly described as a Rayonnant building in the French sense. Yet all three abounded with French ideas, and in the end there emerged in England a late Gothic style, Perpendicular, which was wholly based on the use of tracery panels. Without the influence of France it would be impossible to account for this radical metamorphosis of English Gothic. But with characteristic perverseness Perpendicular was to be in its way every bit as insular as the so-called Early English Gothic of the previous age. It has no counterpart on the European mainland. The only part of England that did contribute something to the stock of late Gothic ideas on the continent was the north. Here the main centre was York, where the nave of the cathedral was rebuilt after 1291. In its own way York, like London, responded to what was happening abroad, although in this case it was perhaps the Low Countries and the Rhineland rather than France which provided the inspiration. But what distinguished the Gothic of northern England in the first half of the 14th century was its tracery. Right from the start English tracery designers showed tremendous inventiveness and, so far as we can tell, they were the first to explore the possibilities of reversing curves, at least in stone. (The sinuous line of the reversed curve would seem more appropriate to a tensile and resilient material like metal rather than stone, and it may well be that the idea was borrowed from metalwork. In that case it

may have originated in the Low Countries, and constitute yet another symptom of interaction between the two arts.) In the great west window of York minster, surely the loveliest thing of its kind in the whole range of Gothic windows, and even more unambiguously in the blind tracery behind the reredos at Beverley, these reversed curves form themselves into characteristic flame-like shapes, which are perhaps better known by the French term '*flamboyant*'. There can be little doubt that there is some connection between these English patterns and the features from which late Gothic in France takes its name. But how the idea was transmitted from England to France is something of a mystery. It is often said that the English invasion of France in the Hundred Years War had something to do with it—as though English soldiers travelled with tracery patterns in their knapsacks. What is perhaps more likely is that the English idea was taken up first in the Low Countries (where it may even have developed on its own) and that it passed from there to France, along with all the other Flemish forms which left their mark on French art at the end of the 14th century.

Be that as it may, the other English contribution, namely patterned vaulting, came from roughly the same part of the world, i.e. the dioceses of York and Lincoln. The asymmetrical vaults of St Hugh's choir at Lincoln were designed as early as 1200, and the star-patterned vaults of the aisles of the nave there (c. 1230) after an interval of more than two generations suddenly appear to have caught the attention of masons working for the Cistercians and the Teutonic Knights in improbably outlandish parts of the world like

78

79
80

79

81

71

82. **Choir of St Vitus cathedral, Prague.** Choir completed 1385. The French architect called in by Charles IV to rebuild Prague cathedral, Matthew of Arras, died in 1352, and his place was taken in 1353 by a German, Peter Parler. He designed the net vaults of the choir, which, unifying as they do the entire vault surface in a continuous pattern, are of great importance to later German decorated vaults.

83. **Franciscan church, Salzburg.** Nave consecrated 1221, choir begun 1408. Hans von Burghausen (or Stethaimer), the architect of the choir, worked on a number of churches in eastern Bavaria and Austria at the end of the 14th century and beginning of the 15th. All are characterised by their great height and complex vaults. This choir at Salzburg is perhaps the most spectacular, thanks to the deliberate contrast between choir and nave.

Pomerania and East Prussia. Just why this should have happened is very hard to say. Nevertheless the event was to be of some importance, for the ideas in question filtered southward through Silesia and reached Prague, the capital of Bohemia, in the 1350s, at the very moment when the cathedral of Prague was being built by a German mason called Peter Parler. There are some indications that Parler knew what was happening in England on his own account. Perhaps after the Hundred Years War broke out German masons, who had formerly spent their *Wanderjahre* learning how the French did things, turned to England instead. But however it happened there came together at Prague two different currents of development, one ultimately from France, the other from England. And from their mixing, under the aegis of the royal patronage of Bohemia, at that time by far the most important in the German world, there emerged the characteristic late Gothic style of Germany.

GOTHIC IN GERMANY

During the 13th century Germany encountered Gothic in two forms—as Rayonnant direct from France, and in the much more primitive version that was favoured by the mendicant orders. As Rayonnant was both expensive and difficult, it was attempted only on special occasions, of which Cologne and the Strasbourg nave provided the most outstanding instances. The very size of these undertakings made them a kind of training ground, where German masons slowly mastered both the methods of Gothic construction and the techniques of tracery design. This early prestige remained with them right through the Middle Ages, and Strasbourg was actually accorded formal pre-eminence over all the masonic lodges in Germany. The friars' churches, though far less impressive as architecture, were important for another reason. The religious condition of Germany in the 13th century offered scope for the friars second only to Italy and Languedoc. And the scale on which they built their churches in Germany was only equalled or surpassed in Italy. The international character of their organisations was responsible for bringing into Germany types of church that were perhaps more at home in the south rather than in the north of Europe, and this may be one of the reasons why the kind of building known as the 'hall church' found favour there in Gothic times. Structurally, the antecedents of the hall church were the single-storeyed Romanesque abbeys of south-west France, Catalonia and perhaps northern Italy. Their defining characteristic was the absence of a clearstorey, and in the Gothic halls this result was achieved by making the aisles as high as the nave. It would not do, however, to stress unduly the friars' predilection for this kind of church. It is perhaps true that for preaching purposes high aisles and broad arcades were more suitable than their opposites, and it is certainly true that some of their more ambitious buildings in the 13th century conformed to the hall church formula. But their patronage of the type was never exclusive, and in any case the prevalence of halls among late Gothic

84. Choir of St Sebaldus, Nürnberg. 1361–72. The
parish church of St Sebaldus was built in the 13th century,
but the choir was rebuilt (possibly by one of the Parler family)
in the 14th in a manner more suited to house the remains of
its patron saint. The choir is a combination of hall church
and chapel, with an ambulatory around the shrine.

churches in Germany requires something more by way of
explanation than the friars can provide.

One way of describing a hall church is to say that it
combines some of the characteristics of a church with a
nave and two aisles, i.e. a cathedral, with some of the characteristics of a chapel. It is in effect a chapel with two rows
of columns inside. During the 14th century we can trace the
development of German thought along these lines until the
hall church emerges as a third alternative. In 1355, when
a new choir was built at Aachen to house the shrine of
Charlemagne, who was treated as a saint in his own church,
it took the form of an attenuated Sainte Chapelle, and it
may be regarded as the German equivalent of the choir of
Gloucester which was also intended to honour a would-be
royal saint. But long before that time, the tall windows
running from floor to vault which are an infallible symptom that Gothic architects were thinking in terms of chapels, whether the Sainte Chapelle or not, had appeared in
the apses of a number of churches, mostly below cathedral
rank, while the rest of the building was handled in the
usual way, i.e. as a basilica. Most of these hybrids are now
to be found in the lower Rhineland and the Low Countries,
but it may be that the idea spread north and east from the
Paris region. In a sense, the hall church was the result of
extending this process of conversion to the rest of the building. Just as it is possible to think of the Sainte Chapelle as an
isolated cathedral clearstorey, so it is possible to see the influence of the high windows of Cologne cathedral in the
Wiesenkirche at Soest, which was built in 1331 by a mason
who was laid off when the choir of Cologne was finished in

1322. Perhaps the Wiesenkirche is not the best example
whereby to illustrate the chapel-like propensities of hall
churches. But in something like the choir of St Sebaldus at
Nürnberg (1361), these are quite unmistakable. Outside it
is an enlarged Sainte Chapelle, while inside it is a hall, with
the shrine of St Sebaldus himself still there to underline the
symbolic function of the whole building. Moreover, if we
turn to the choir of the Franciscan church at Salzburg
which, although it belongs to the first decade of the 15th
century, really forms an integral part of this development,
we shall see just how seriously the master-mason, Hans von
Burghausen, set about the task of making us conscious of the
spatial unity of his hall. Although there are columns, they
do not form bays; and if we compare his vault with that of
the Wiesenkirche, we observe that the latter is conceived as
a series of discrete compartments, whereas the former has
an all-over pattern as though it were an encrusted ceiling.
There is perhaps no more fitting monument than the choir
at Salzburg at which to break off these remarks on late German Gothic architecture. Designed deliberately as a foil to
the dark and low 13th-century nave by which it is approached, its soaring space and brilliant light can still evoke
vestiges of the piety and fervour that converged on the altar
in its midst. It may well be that what we have here is no
longer a victory monument of the Church Triumphant, as
at Chartres. But perhaps there is something more than
poetry in those German eulogies which see in this and similar buildings a vision permeated by the higher spirituality
of the later Middle Ages.

But before we leave Gothic architecture altogether, there

85. **West tower of Ulm minster.** 15th and 19th centuries.
86. **West front of Laon cathedral.** Late 12th century. Laon (see also figure 61) was built with towers not only at the west end, but also at the crossing and over the transepts. This fashion for a large number of towers (compare figure 28) gave way in the High Gothic period to a preference for two west towers alone. In the later Middle Ages often all attention was focused on a single enormous tower of elaborate design, such as this example at Ulm, the upper parts of which were only completed (in accordance with the medieval architect's drawings) in the 19th century. Contrast these two examples of Gothic design with the Romanesque towers of Cluny and La Charité sur Loire (figures 27, 28).

are two more of its many aspects to which allusion, however brief, must be made. One of these is the part played by towers and spires in the external effects of the great churches of the north. Up to a point it is true to say that all the really interesting things about later Gothic are concerned with surface decoration of one kind or another. Even vaults, which began as structural devices *par excellence* ended up as overhead surface patterns, different in 78, 82 detail from window tracery perhaps, but not serving any essentially different aesthetic purpose. Indeed, the fan vaults of English Perpendicular were to all intents and purposes tracery applied to the surface of the vault. When structural variations were adopted they were nearly always simplifications of the High Gothic system. The one exception to this rule was the great church tower, which was generally intended to carry a spire as well, although it did not always receive one. The idea of the great tower was inherited from Romanesque architecture, and no doubt to 27, 28 begin with they performed the same functions in a Gothic as in a Romanesque church, i.e. at the west end to carry bells and to provide useful rooms for storage, and over the crossing to serve as lanterns (though this was not always the case). They were of course also intended to make imposing façades, and to provide, when present, suitably climactic effects at the centre of the building. But Gothic towers seem to have gradually shed their practical aspects in favour of symbolic ones. The crucial moment was probably reached when the architect of Laon decided to build his towers 86 open. No doubt there were good practical reasons for doing this. For one thing, the superstructure could be made a good deal lighter, and all sorts of complications at the corners could be made much more effective than in a solid tower. But the principal effect of the change was to substitute a gigantic free-standing ciborium for what had hitherto been a box, and this allowed the tower to acquire something of the iconographical significance of the individual compartments of the building below. It is clear from the remarks by Villard de Honnecourt on the subject that the towers of Laon made a great stir, and the methods used there to effect the transition from a square to an octagonal section continued in use right down to the end of the Middle Ages. Until the time when the façade of Strasbourg was designed (*c.* 1277), towers and spires tended to become more and more delicate, so that in the end they seemed more like the fantasies of metalworkers than structures of 85 solid stone. It is a great pity that the Strasbourg towers

87. **Nave of Barcelona cathedral.** Begun 1298. The huge arcades resting on lofty piers—a feature of both Barcelona cathedral and the slightly later church of Sta Maria del Mar in the same town (plate 62)—are reminiscent of the design of Bourges (plate 59) but the dim interior is typical of the Gothic of southern Europe (compare figure 67).

were never built on the lines laid down in the famous drawing, but we can get some idea of what they might have been like from the lantern and open-work spire at Freiburg, further up the Rhine (started *c.* 1300). Shortly afterwards, however, in the façade designed for Cologne cathedral (*c.* 1330), everything was enlarged to a gigantic scale. Spires over five hundred feet high were planned, and to ensure their stability many more stages, and therefore sections and set-backs, were required. Towers of this magnitude called for engineering skills of perhaps an even higher order than those demonstrated for us by the vaults of the 13th-century cathedrals. In Germany they became something of a masonic *tour de force*, and as prestige symbols 85 their value was no doubt overwhelming. Of the many that were designed, however, only two were actually completed during the Middle Ages—the great monolithic finger on the west front of Strasbourg (which replaced the earlier design), and the south tower at Vienna. But their counterparts exist in every country of northern Europe.

It is necessary to resist the temptation to regard these towers merely as vulgar prodigies. In the multitude of gables by which they are surrounded at all levels, the idea of the niche is never very far away, and each of the finials that terminate the residual masonry at the set-backs is in a sense a miniature tower and spire in itself. The spire of Strasbourg is made up of tier upon tier of open traceried compartments, in fact a veritable multitude of tiny ciboria. No statues inhabit these abodes, but this is perhaps no more than the recognition of inexpediency. On the Tour de Beurre at Rouen, which is one of the best French examples, clusters of statues may be seen high up and far away from the eye of any human beholder, each under his own gable—the saints keeping their eternal watch. And this, basically, is the purpose that all the niches and gables were meant to serve. In the last resort the tower itself was a gigantic reliquary, the last and in some ways the greatest of the medieval variations on this theme.

This brings us back once more to the recurrent question of interaction among the Gothic arts. In the cathedral 66 treasury at Aachen are two magnificent reliquaries, each in the form of three towers. They date from the middle of the 14th century and, scale, material and technique apart, it is clear that there is a fundamental identity of form between them and, say, the towers and spires of the Strasbourg drawing. The largest and the smallest categories of Gothic art meet in their preoccupation with the symbolism of the 69, 75 niche. The formula could be applied in many ways. King Edward II of England at Gloucester (d. 1327) and Pope John XXII at Avignon (d. 1334) both lie under their own, stone, versions of the Three Towers shrine. Gabled can- 68 opies of wood could be placed side by side to form choir-stalls, or enlarged in splendid isolation to make a bishop's throne, so that in yet another way during the performance of the holy office the clergy could feel themselves at one

with the company of Heaven. In stained glass and in illuminated manuscripts ornamental architecture of the same kind serves precisely the same purpose, and it was almost certainly with the intention of evoking an illusion of this sacred space under canopies that the first tentative steps were taken in the north toward the mastery of perspective.

The versatility and often the sheer banality of so much of this Gothic niche-work is apt to deflect the attention of amateurs toward the exceptional masterpieces, which qualify as art to us. But for any historical estimate this was what Gothic art was really about—the evocation of the sacred. By far the most effective way of doing this was by drawing lines of demarcation between the sacred and the profane, i.e. by setting space apart, or devoting it, in the old classical sense of the word. This has always been architecture's special function, and there is nothing remarkable in Gothic acknowledgment of the fact. But the scope of the idea was something that the Middle Ages had to explore for themselves, and behind the tortuous proliferation of Gothic detail may be detected the strong flavour of a very peculiar yet not wholly preposterous religiosity.

GOTHIC IN SOUTHERN EUROPE

It is against the background of this all-pervading aspect of northern Gothic that we ought finally to turn once more to the south. For there the prickly paraphernalia of Gothic tracery and niche-work is for the most part conspicuous by its absence. When we do come across it, as at Milan (1386) and the later Gothic cathedrals of Spain (e.g. 15th-century Seville) we may be certain that masons from Germany, the Low Countries or France have been travelling far from home. But at Albi (1282) the predominant impression of the masonry is that of the bleak Dominican church at Toulouse, and perhaps it was even closer to the lost Franciscan church there which was even more severe. In Aragón the same austerity was combined with a still more ambitious type of structure. The 14th-century cathedral of Palma de Mallorca, and Sta Maria del Mar at Barcelona, perhaps the most spectacular Gothic building in the western Mediterranean, confront us with distinct allusions to the programme of Bourges. Here if anywhere the great Gothic tradition of structural engineering was carried beyond the achievements of 13th-century France. The ultimate triumph of Gothic vaulting, the projection of a span of more than seventy feet across the nave of Gerona, was reserved for Catalonia. And it is perhaps worth remembering that the debate of the Gerona masons as to whether they should attempt this prodigious feat took place at almost exactly the same time as another debate at Florence, where Brunelleschi tried to persuade the masons of the cathedral that it was possible to build the projected dome bequeathed to them by their predecessors. In conception if not in execution, that dome was a Gothic work, and Florence cathedral (started 1296) belongs to a group of Italian churches which, though on the whole less enterprising than their Aragonese counterparts, reflect much the same general approach to Gothic. Sta Maria Novella at Florence (nave 1278) is perhaps the most satisfying of these, but Milan cathedral (before it received the benefits of northern cooperation) and S. Petronio, Bologna (started 1390), are its most grandiose representatives.

There is certainly no lack of competence in these southern Gothic buildings, and if the forms of northern decoration are missing this must ultimately be a question of southern taste. But it also follows that the role of the masons in the general economy of the arts was very different in the south. By the 14th century Gothic had come to mean two quite distinct things, which can be summarised under the headings of engineering and design. In the north both were practised by the same people, whereas in the south the masons did the engineering and decoration was left to someone else, usually painters. The fact that in Italy the exponents and guardians of the traditions of 'disegno' were not primarily architects was certainly responsible in part for the eccentric development of all the arts there in the 14th and 15th centuries. For one thing, the masons, because they had no vocabulary of architectural ornament of their own, were wide open to Brunelleschi's classicism when it came. And in fact all the really interesting things in late Florentine Gothic are concerned with the search for just such a vocabulary. But the most important thing of all

was the undue prominence that painting assumed in Italy. The invention of linear perspective might almost be said to have arisen from the efforts of painters to do what in the north would have been left to the niche-workers. The creation of the illusion of space was first and foremost a question of creating an illusion of architecture. But before we consider the significance of Gothic painting it is necessary to say something about the figure arts, and first and foremost this means sculpture.

GOTHIC SCULPTURE

If we go right back to St Denis, we come face to face with a preliminary paradox that the sculpture of the first Gothic buildings can only really be called Romanesque. New beginnings in architecture do not necessarily mean new beginnings in sculpture and, so far as we can tell, the transformation of the figure arts started in a region notorious for its loyalty to Romanesque architecture. Furthermore it would be quite wrong to postulate some pre-ordained course of parallel development for the two arts. By the 1170s the new architecture and the new figure sculpture met up with one another, probably in Champagne, and from then on they proceeded to develop in close proximity to one another for about a hundred years. But to speak of Gothic sculpture before about 1230 requires a good deal of qualification.

The great discovery made by the sculptors of the High Gothic cathedrals was that the special relationship between God and man could be expressed in terms of man alone, and that neither the divinity of God nor the experience of God required any drastic transfiguration of the human form. Henceforth both God and the saints could be depicted without conspicuous stylistic deformation, and for the first time since classical antiquity the way was open for a kind of art that was both humanist and representa-

88 (opposite). **St John the Baptist.**
c. 1215. South doorway on the west front
of Reims cathedral. The rebuilding of
Reims cathedral began in 1211, and
from the beginning an extensive
sculptural programme was planned.
Some of the earliest figures are the
forerunners of Christ of whom *St John the
Baptist* is one. Stylistically they can be
linked with the north transept sculptures
of Chartres.

89. **The Blessed in Heaven.** 1230s.
Tympanum of the Christ Porch in the
north transept of Reims cathedral. The
serenity of these figures is typical of the
idealised view of mankind which
characterises so much of early 13th-
century French sculpture. While the
Germans aimed at representing man's
emotional reaction to a situation, the
French in such sculptures as these
achieved a heroic quality of a totally
different nature.

tional. It is not surprising, therefore, that in emancipating
themselves from the tyranny of attitudes which had prevailed since Early Christian times, Gothic sculptors should
have called upon classical forms, or what they took to be
classical forms, to play a catalytic role. They did so in
several stages. It was brilliantly demonstrated recently
that in the north portal of the west front of Notre Dame,
Paris, the style of the column figures was more than superficially affected by 10th-century Byzantine ideas, perhaps
an indirect consequence of the flood of portable Byzantine
works of art that reached the West after the sack of the city
by the Crusaders of 1204. But more or less at the same time,
i.e. about 1220, the first group of sculptors working at
Reims took the even more decisive step of using actual
Roman statues as their models. In view of what happened
in Paris, it is unlikely that the Master of the Antique Fig-
63 ures at Reims expressly wished his *Virgin of the Visitation* to
look like a Roman matron. Instead we ought perhaps to
see both sets of statues as attempts to find suitable formulas
for free-standing figures, by men who were not yet clear in
their own minds as to what they wanted and did not want
their images to be. To us, knowing that in another two
hundred years sculptors would once more turn to the antique for their inspiration, the early works at Reims are
liable to seem unduly significant. That they were perhaps
the most accomplished statues of their generation cannot
be denied. But the most important thing about them is that
101 in spite of their quality they were not copied (except at
Bamberg). The second school of Reims sculptors evolved
89 an entirely new style of drapery which owed nothing to its
predecessors, apart from a certain sense of monumentality,
and perhaps the method of building up figures from simple
geometrical abstractions. In the abrupt end which befell
this brief Gothic experiment with classical sculpture it is
possible to recognise once more the censorship of the

Church. At the moment when the Inquisition was setting
up its tribunals, it is hardly likely that classical forms should
seem anything other than pagan. But in any case the pro-
hibition, if it amounted to such, cannot be said to have
frustrated the natural growth of Gothic sculpture.

While it is clear that the imitation human being was in
some sense the goal at which sculptors were aiming, it
would be wrong to regard this quest as an exact replica of
that which led the Greeks from archaic to classical forms.
For the Greeks the human ideal could be expressed only in
terms of physical perfection. For the men of the Middle
Ages, however, with their acute sense of the antithesis between body and soul, humanism was first and foremost concerned with the attributes of personality. All virtue belonged to the soul, and the vitality of the soul was expressed
through the emotions. In so far as it sought to render these
things in movement, gesture and facial expression, Gothic 72,90
sculpture was much closer to its Hellenistic than to its classical antecedents. But in practice it received very little help
from any examples. The sculptors were on their own, and
the novelty of their enterprise, especially in its early stages,
revealed itself in both understatement and overemphasis.

Essentially the problems resolved themselves into two
quite distinct categories. On the one hand were those connected with the rendering of things like beauty, grace, 89
nobility or wisdom—the ideal aspects of personality—
while on the other were less edifying characteristics and the 90
more extreme forms of emotion. At the risk of committing
a gross oversimplification, it is expedient to deal with these
separately, and to discuss the former as though they were
exclusively French, and the latter as though they were predominantly German. It may be said at once that neither of
these generalisations is true, but the accidents of survival to
some extent excuse this cavalier treatment. They also justify taking the German achievements first.

90. **The Last Judgment.** Second quarter of the 13th century. North portal *(Fürstenportal)* of Bamberg cathedral. Instead of presenting a catalogue of possible torments the sculptor of this tympanum set out to portray the emotional reaction of those condemned to everlasting damnation. Ludicrous as the result may seem in this case, the attempt to enhance a dramatic situation through its emotional content is of great importance to German sculpture.

92 (opposite). **The Death of the Virgin.** Second quarter of the 14th century. South transept portal, Strasburg cathedral. Although both in facial types and drapery styles these figures from one of the tympana show affinities with contemporary French sculpture, the dramatic presentation of the scene is characteristically German.

91. **South transept portal of Strasbourg cathedral.** Second quarter of the 13th century. The Gothic figures set on either side of this Romanesque portal represent the *Church* and the *Synagogue*. Although each has her traditional attributes, the postures of the two figures are themselves expressive of triumph and defeat. The trumeau figure represents Solomon.

Between about 1230 and 1260 three programmes of sculpture were carried out in Germany of surprising virtuosity. They were at the cathedrals of Bamberg, Strasbourg and Naumburg. Although the Master of Naumburg was active after the reception of Rayonnant architecture on the Rhineland, all three are associated with buildings whose Gothic is either nonexistent or of an extremely tentative kind, which makes the High Gothic connections of the sculptors themselves even more remarkable. Before these campaigns there was comparatively little monumental sculpture to be seen in Germany, and what there was seems to have emanated from Italy rather than France. The dramatic shift of German interest from the south to what was happening beyond the Rhine after the battle of Bouvines in 1214, and after the virtual withdrawal of Imperial patronage, is symptomatic of the new political and cultural orientations of 13th-century Europe. It might have been expected that this decline in the political fortunes of Germany would have entailed a general atrophy of her spiritual life. On the contrary, in certain fields, precisely the opposite happened. A generation before, German poetry had suddenly burst into life, and it is perhaps legitimate to acknowledge bonds of sympathy between the poets and the sculptors, even though their statues were not meant to illustrate literature. Why should we not think of Wolfram's *Parsifal* when we look at the Bamberg *Rider*?

71,72, 90,91

BAMBERG

The impact of French sculpture on Germany can perhaps best be seen at Bamberg. Already before the exponents of

the new style arrived, a screen around the eastern choir was being carved in a late Romanesque style of tremendous vigour, seemingly derived from contemporary Bavarian manuscripts, as one might have expected in a region without established traditions of monumental sculpture. The French influences came from Reims, but they seem to have been infused by the vitality of the local school in more ways than one. Although they are connected, the freedom and energy of the Bamberg drapery folds make the efforts of the *101* Master of the Antique Figures at Reims seem pedantic by *63* comparison. This vigour is a token of a quite different artistic purpose. In nearly all the great ensembles of French cathedral sculpture the overriding purpose is didactic. The figures are there to represent nothing more than themselves in the concourse of the heavenly host. Often they can be identified only by their attributes. But the Bamberg Master on his infinitely smaller scale is concerned with something more, which might be called the emotional participation of his characters. From this point of view he is at his most interesting, even if he is not entirely successful, *90* when he tries to cope with a dramatic scene like the *Last* *89* *Judgment*. On the whole, French *Last Judgments* tend to be phlegmatic affairs, which only come to life, so to speak, in the horrible torments of the damned. At Bamberg we are offered not scenes of damnation but what are meant to be contrasted psychological studies of the saved and the damned. The contrast is admittedly not very effective. If the little souls on their way to the eternal delights of Abraham's bosom look suitably smug, those about to suffer seem in positive transports of hilarity. The attempt to con-

vey anguish has misfired. But the important thing is that it should have been attempted at all.

STRASBOURG

At Strasbourg, hardly any later than Bamberg (*c.* 1235), nothing whatever has misfired. On the south transept of the cathedral are two portals, each with a carved tympanum, *91* one devoted to the death of the Virgin, the other to her coronation. The *Coronation* scene is handled in a perfunctory way in a style which, though reminiscent of Chartres, could equally well have been derived from the famous *Hortus Deliciarum*, a manuscript closely connected with Nicholas of Verdun, and at that time kept at the monastery of Mont Ste Odile, near Strasbourg. On the other hand, the *Death of the Virgin* is so shot through with sentimentality *92* that it would seem almost more at home in the 19th century than in the 13th. The traditional Byzantine formula, where Christ himself comes to carry the Virgin's soul to heaven, has been turned into a purely human death-bed scene in which the Son pays his last respects to his mother, and the row of apostles in the background provide an array of expressions of muted grief. Even the malignant Jew in the foreground has been rendered in an equivocal way so as not to strike a discordant note. One may not approve of this kind of art today, but it shows a remarkable command of the technique of arousing emotion by representing it which, after all, has been one of the principal methods of Western art from that time almost to our own.

When we turn to the statues of the *Church* and the *Synagogue* which stand on either side of the Strasbourg portals,

93. **Synagogue.** Second quarter of the 13th century. South transept porch, Strasbourg cathedral. The anatomical distortions of this figure, which are exaggerated by the clinging draperies, convey, as the impassive face does not, a sense of defeat. The eloquent twist of the body, and the head averted from her triumphant rival, the *Church*, are echoed in the multiple breaks in the spear she carries.

the possibilities of sculpture seem to have been explored a stage further. The contrast between these two symbols was a specialised form of a dichotomy on which Romanesque theologians had meditated endlessly—that between old and new, prophets and apostles, nature and grace, and so on. The *Church* is a beautiful young woman with cross and chalice, looking boldly across the portal at her superseded rival. The *Synagogue* is also a beautiful young woman—at least from the front. Her head is downcast and turned against the twist of her body, so that one senses a certain tension in her acquiescence. But if we actually look at her from the side, that is as the *Church* sees her, everything changes. It is from this angle that the broken spear really looks broken, the downcast head is on a broken neck, and the lovely body turns out to have an ugly sag in the abdomen. Like Kundry in *Parsifal* this image has two personalities, one beautiful and one repulsive; the beautiful one is a snare of worldliness, while the ugly one is the truth as God sees it. Is this reading too much into a Gothic statue? If it were an isolated case, it would be as well to be sceptical. But at Naumburg the beholder is brought into an even more specific relationship with a statue, or rather with a group of statues.

NAUMBURG

The west choir of the cathedral of Naumburg seems to have been built, either just before or just after 1249, as a kind of memorial chapel ostensibly intended to honour early benefactors of the cathedral. This choir or chapel is closed off from the rest of the church by a screen which is carved with reliefs of the Passion. It was customary in medieval churches to raise over the screen dividing choir and nave a rood cross, i.e. a crucifixion, with Mary and St John in attendance. A few Romanesque examples have survived in Germany, and there are several famous painted instances from Italy. The imagery that surrounded the rood cross was particularly complex, and in 13th-century Germany it was often presented in a lavish and literal way. The Naumburg instance is only the best preserved. Here the rood has been brought down and placed in the doorway of the screen, so that the doors are set under the arms of the cross. Anyone entering the chapel has therefore to pass immediately under the outstretched arms of Christ. The idea that Christ was the door to everlasting life may be found in many French cathedrals, but usually in the form of the *Beau Dieu* of Chartres which, if nothing else, is infinitely less theatrical. The *Christ* at Naumburg is deliberately pathetic. The crown of thorns hurts. The body twists with pain. He is a human being, dying. The Romanesque roods completely ignored this aspect of the crucifixion. They present the death of Christ as a triumph. Sometimes, as in the Ottonian Gero cross at Cologne, one senses the heroic cost, but pathos is always absent. The Naumburg *Christ* is the first known to us in which it becomes the predominant aspect. By comparison with the extravagant variations on the theme which followed and

which did not reach their culmination until Grünewald's Isenheim altarpiece in the 16th century, it is modest and passive, and all the more moving. We cannot escape this Christ. On either side of the doorway are the lamenting figures of Mary and St John who point to him in their grief, which in this case cannot be mistaken for anything else. But Mary goes further. She is not wrapped up in her grief. She lays one hand on her breast, points to Christ with the other and addresses you, the beholder. You are brought dramatically into the situation.

The whole thing is in fact a little Passion play. And the scenes in relief above are stills from the same drama. Whether they were in fact inspired by some primitive Oberammergau, they achieve an unprecedented realism. The sculptor delights in capturing the most ephemeral gestures—drinking from a cup at the Last Supper, or even pouring the water for Pilate to wash his hands. The figures move with a solemn prescience as though they know they have to reveal their characters in their faces. We recognise the forbearance of Christ, the malignance of the High Priest and the weakness of Pilate. Although these scenes had been carved on many previous occasions, this was perhaps the first time that the figures were set out in depth, in a way reminiscent of later pictures.

Inside the choir, somewhat to our surprise, we encounter realism of quite another sort. It is clear that the sculptor was acutely sensitive to the tragedy of the Passion, and he may well have been the kind of artist who expressed his piety through his art. But this does not prepare us for the assortment of secular characters who await us. Moreover, the discovery that they are all historical personalities adds to the surprise. As they all lived and died long before the statues were made, there is no possibility that they were literal portraits. But they could have been modelled on actual contemporaries, and they inevitably call to mind characters from contemporary literature. With the possible exception of a lively Frenchman masquerading as St Joseph at Reims, these are the first medieval statues about which we may risk remarks on the subject of national character. Germans say that they are unmistakably German, and few would disagree, at least about some of them.

It is not necessary to actually like the Master of Naumburg's work to realise his importance. In his quest for realism at all costs he was obviously a fanatic, but in finding ways to achieve his purpose he broke new ground. For this man art was not primarily a question of making the invisible visible, or simply of making statues. It was making people. The dangers to which this point of view could lead he managed to avoid, either because he was an innovator, or because he lived and worked in an aristocratic world. But we can trace his influence through a succession of later German sculptors who, perhaps to suit the taste of burgher patrons, turned his expressiveness into caricature. On the one hand there are horrible things like the Pestkreuz at St Maria im Kapitol at Cologne, which is a veritable anticipation of Grünewald, on the other the mannered and slightly

72

73

74

94. **Gero Crucifix.** Third quarter of the 10th century. h. 74 in. (188 cm.). Wood with traces of pigmentation. Cologne cathedral. Compare this stern Ottonian interpretation of the Crucifixion (see also plate 15) with the Gothic sculpture at Naumburg (figure 95).

95. **The Naumburg Master.** *The Crucifixion.* After 1249. Rood screen, Naumburg cathedral. The expressive figures of the Virgin and St John in this Crucifixion group convey their emotions with a dignity and restraint which is far more realistic than the exaggerated contortions of the Bamberg damned (figure 90).

96 (left). **Nicola Pisano.** *The Crucifixion* (detail). 1260. Detail of pulpit in Pisa Baptistery.
98 (opposite). **Giovanni Pisano.** *The Crucifixion* (detail). 1301. Detail of pulpit in S. Andrea, Pistoia. The striking difference in style between these works by two members of the same family can only be explained by the influence on Giovanni Pisano of northern Gothic sculpture. Although the placing of the figures in both details is almost identical, the stiff poses and classically-inspired heads of Nicola's group have a formality which, in Giovanni's work, has been replaced by a feeling for movement and expression more compatible with the art of the Master of Naumburg (see figure 95). (See also plate 75.)

97. **Claus Sluter.** *Head of Christ.* 1395–9. Stone. h. 24 in. (61 cm.). Musée Archéologique, Dijon. This fragment of the *Crucified Christ* comes from the Calvary which originally surmounted Sluter's Well of Moses, executed for the Chartreuse de Champmol at Dijon between 1395 and 1406. This sculpture, though mutilated, is still an impressive portrayal of patient suffering.

frivolous statues in the west portals at Strasbourg. It needed *99* an artist endowed with very great depth of feeling and acute sense of character to control this legacy, and so far as the north of Europe was concerned there was apparently no one of the requisite calibre before Sluter at the end of the 14th century. It is doubtful whether Sluter actually knew any of the Master of Naumburg's work, although it is conceivable that he may have seen some at Mainz. But either knowingly or unknowingly, when Sluter cut right across the fashionable delicate style of his day in favour of monumental figures, highly charged with emotion, he was taking up where the Master of Naumburg left off. The head and torso of *Christ* from Sluter's Calvary at Dijon *97* (1395) is the first to bear comparison with the Naumburg *95* *Christ*, while the *Virgin and Child* from the portal of the Chartreuse at Dijon remind us, if not of the Naumburg *Virgin* herself, then of the essays on that theme by the Italian, Giovanni Pisano.

THE PISANO FAMILY

If anyone can be said to have inherited the outlook of the Master of Naumburg, the best claimant in the generation that followed was this most gifted member of a whole dynasty of sculptors. Giovanni's father, Nicola, appeared at Pisa in the middle years of the 13th century, where he completed a pulpit for the Baptistery in 1260. It is often said that he came from the south of Italy, where Emperor Frederick II (1198–1250) had been promoting his own private renaissance for political ends. Frederick's activities constituted the one blatant instance of outright 'pagan'

classicism in the Middle Ages. At Capua in 1233, on a monumental gateway guarding the approaches to the River Volturno on the road from papal Rome, whose lower section was composed of superbly rusticated masonry, were several statues and busts in niches representing the Emperor and his officers of state accompanied by allegorical figures whose purpose certainly fell under the heading of propaganda. Togas, fillets and ideal facial features, together with a quite unmedieval sense of anatomical proportions, set these statues apart even from the classicising works at Reims. Not unnaturally they have been hailed as harbingers of the later Italian Renaissance. Yet in their own time, with the possible exception of Nicola Pisano, they were curiously without influence, and like everything else about him Frederick's use of classical art forms is shrouded in ambiguity. One suspects that it was nothing more than a convenient instrument of ideological warfare. Certainly for the rooms of his castles, e.g. Castel del Monte (c. 1240), he was prepared to use the prevailing Gothic fashion of his time. Even here, however, it was perversely characteristic of the man to use Gothic for domestic rather than ecclesiastical purposes.

The rusticated masonry of Capua and Castel del Monte reminds us of one other much neglected aspect of medieval classicism, namely its influence on military architecture. When the Crusaders built their castles, e.g. Krak des Chevaliers in Syria, on the principle of two concentric walls each furnished with projecting towers, they were following the example of the 5th-century land walls at Constantinople. No doubt the state of warfare in the 12th and

13th centuries offered highly practical excuses for such imitations. But the castles and fortified defences which the Savoyard, Master James of St George, built for Edward I of England in north Wales about 1280 must have borne an equally remarkable likeness to other late Roman defence works.

But, to return to Italy and the Pisani, the only classical models that come readily to mind when we are confronted by Nicola Pisano's pulpit are Etruscan tombs and a sarcophagus known to have been in the Campo Santo at Pisa in his time. So the southern hypothesis is not particularly strong. The Pisa pulpit more or less coincides with the high-water mark of Imperial fortunes in central Italy, i.e. the victory of Montaperti in 1260. And with the triumph of the papal agent, the Frenchman Charles of Anjou, over the Hohenstaufen in 1265 it soon evaporated. The three successors of the Pisa pulpit, made for the cathedral of Siena (1265), S. Andrea at Pistoia (finished 1301) and the cathedral at Pisa (finished 1310), have a much more pronounced northern Gothic flavour. It is often said that Giovanni, who was responsible for much of the second and all the last two pulpits, learnt his Gothic in France. It may well be that he went to France, but if he did so he almost certainly went via the Rhineland, and the religious hysteria that seems to animate his later work is much more likely to have been imbibed in Germany than in France. Even so, it is not necessary to attribute all his violence and agitation to northern sources. If he ever saw something like a 3rd-century AD battle sarcophagus (now in the Ludovisi collection of the Terme Museum at Rome) this could well

99. **Prophets.** Last quarter of the 13th century. Central portal on the west front of Strasbourg cathedral. The draperies of these figures, which give little indication of the body beneath, and the elaborate treatment of hair and beards are symptomatic of a swing in interest away from the heroic forms of early 13th-century sculpture and towards that absorption with decorative detail which marks so much 14th-century work.

have accounted for more than just the formal lay-out of his panels. Other members of the Pisano family, less emotional than Giovanni, did, however, derive from France a more congenial kind of Gothic. The first set of bronze doors, which Andrea Pisano made for the Baptistery at Florence (1330), brings us face to face with the more suave and elegant Gothic figure style whose ultimate home was Paris.

In discussing this German Gothic sculpture, and works that share its fundamental outlook, the vocabulary of human experience comes naturally to mind. The function of drapery in these statues is subordinate to, and in fact shows off, their psychological content. Nevertheless a Gothic statue was very seldom thought of as a body over which draperies happened to have been placed, as classical Greek statues were. For most Gothic sculptors drapery was the body. Just how essential clothes were becomes painfully obvious when they were removed altogether, which is what happened to the embarrassed but celebrated *Adam and Eve* at Bamberg—the first monumental nudes in medieval art. As examples of anatomy they are woefully inadequate, however effective as reminders of original sin. When

we turn to the other main category of Gothic figures, however, where there was no ulterior purpose for the drapery to serve, we find that the patterns tended to become ends in themselves. Actually no very hard and fast line of demarcation can be drawn between the two groups in this respect. The same conventions could obviously occur on both sides of the line.

The first essential was for monumental figures to emancipate themselves from the influence of the columns out of which they had, so to speak, emerged. We find symptoms of this in the transept and portals at Chartres, where the figures begin to loosen and turn towards one another. At Reims by 1220 the process was complete. A decided swaying movement can be detected in some figures of the classical group, and this even operates in the orthogonal dimension as well (i.e. from back to front) although here one suspects that questions of balance and stability were involved, rather than aesthetic effects. How these figures

(Continued on page 161)

84. **School of Giotto.** *St Francis
renouncing his Inheritance. c.* 1300. Upper
church, S. Francesco, Assisi. The drama of
this episode in St Francis's life is
heightened by the sharp demarcation
between the two groups (see p. 165) and
the arrested movement of the figure
stepping towards the saint. The buildings
are seen as three-dimensional objects, and
the bodies of the figures are clearly defined
under their draperies.

85. **Giotto.** *St Francis renouncing his Inheritance.* 1320s. Fresco. Bardi chapel, Sta Croce, Florence.

86. **School of Giotto.** *St Francis driving out the Devils from Arezzo.* c. 1300. Upper church, S. Francesco, Assisi. The very obvious symbolic division of the Assisi frescoes (see plates 86 and 84) has in the later Bardi chapel fresco (plate 85) been rejected in favour of a more subtle composition. The single massive building underlines the emotional conflict of the two groups, and draws the spectator into the centre of the drama. In the Assisi fresco of the casting out of devils the eye is led from one side to the other through the up-flung arm of St Francis.

87. **Duccio.** *The Agony in the Garden*, and
The Betrayal of Judas. Panel from the
Maestà. 1308–11. Museo del'Opera del
Duomo, Siena. When the *Maestà*, to which
this panel belongs, was completed in 1311,
it was carried to Siena cathedral in a
triumphal procession. The soft folds of the
drapery display Duccio's interest in
achieving a decorative effect, very
different from Giotto's starker
monumentality. (See also plate 88.)

88. **Duccio.** *The Entry into Jerusalem.*
Panel from the *Maestà.* 1308–11. Museo
del'Opera del Duomo, Siena. The
composition of this panel conveys a strong
sense of recession. The spectator is led in
through the little gate, to converge with
the crowd spilling out from the town
behind, without a break between foreground and background.

89, 90. **North Italian school.** *Pentecost* (f. 448v), and *Measuring the Heavenly Jerusalem* (f. 473r). From the Bible of Clement VII (MS. 47672). Mid 14th century. 14 × 9½ in. (36 × 24 cm.). British Museum, London. In the Pentecost scene the artist has tried to convey a feeling of depth by seating the apostles and Virgin in a box-like room. This kind of spatial experimenting led ultimately to the mastery of perspective in the 15th century. The scene from the Revelation of St John the Divine shows the angel with the golden reed measuring the heavenly Jerusalem. Whereas Duccio's earthly Jerusalem (plate 88) is recognisably an Italian town, this city is a shrine in which the medieval love of precious materials could indulge itself in a literal illustration of St John's description.

91 (opposite, above). **Krak des Chevaliers,** Syria. Late 12th century. This crusader castle, built by the Hospitallers to guard the coastal parts of the Holy Land, on a scale unparalleled by contemporary fortifications in western Europe, includes the revolutionary feature of a double curtain wall. It withstood numerous Muslim sieges until it fell through treachery in 1271.

92 (opposite, below). **Warkworth castle,** Northumberland. 15th century. The keep of Warkworth was rebuilt by the Percy family in the early 15th century. With its symmetrical exterior and complex interior plan, it is not merely a defensive building, but displays the concern for elaborate and comfortable living conditions which increasingly characterises late medieval secular architecture.

93 (above). **Bishop's palace, St Davids.** 13th and 14th centuries. The enormous scale of this Bishop's palace reflects the size and importance of the domestic buildings of medieval ecclesiastical institutions, of which now so often only the churches remain intact. In the later Middle Ages Bishops were frequently criticised for spending too much on their own comfort.

94 (previous pages). **Jean Bondol.**
Apocalypse Tapestry. Begun 1377. h.
169¼ in. (430 cm.). Musée des
Tapisseries, Angers. This scene, of the
woman crowned with the sun, forms part
of a set of tapestries ordered by Louis I of
Anjou for the hall of his castle. Jean
Bondol, who executed the cartoons, was
court painter to Charles V, and even in
the medium of tapestry his quality as an
illuminator is apparent.

95 (above). **William Torel.** *Queen
Eleanor.* 1291–2. Bronze. Approximately
life-size. Westminster abbey. Soon after
the death of Eleanor of Castile in 1290,
Edward I, inspired by the royal tombs at
St Denis, commissioned three bronze
effigies from the goldsmith William Torel
—two of Eleanor herself, and one of
Henry III. In this idealised figure of the
queen there is no attempt at portraiture.

96. **Guy de Dammartin.** *Fireplace in the palace of the Counts of Poitou*, Poitiers. 1384–6. This magnificent triple fireplace with its balustraded gallery was ordered by John, Duke of Berry, one of the wealthiest courtiers and connoisseurs of his time. Between the traceried gables are set figures, not of the saints, but of John of Berry himself, his brother Charles V and their wives.

97 (above). **Tomb effigy of Edward II.**
Early 1330s. Alabaster. Approximately
life-size. Gloucester cathedral. Edward II
was murdered in 1327 and the
splendour of his tomb at Gloucester may
well have been part of the attempt to
surround his besmirched reputation with
the odour of sanctity. The softness of the
alabaster enhances this extremely

romantic image of the king, and the
technical quality of the carving suggests
London workmanship.

98 (opposite). Attributed to **Arnolfo di
Cambio.** *Charles of Anjou. c.* 1277.
Marble. Over life-size. Capitoline
Museum, Rome. This figure, which
commemorates Charles's senatorship of

Rome, is assumed to have stood on the
Capitol. It shows the classical elements, so
marked in the work of Nicola Pisano, in
whose workshop Arnolfo di Cambio was
trained. These still persisted in Italian
Gothic sculpture, side by side with
Giovanni Pisano's developments towards a
style more closely allied with northern
Gothic (see plate 75, figures 96, 98).

ILLE EGO PRECLARI TVLERAM QVI SCEPTRA SENI
REX SICVLIS CAROLVS AVR
OBRVTVS

99. **Bonino da Campione.** *Monument to Cansignorio della Scala.* 1370–4. Sagrato di Sta Maria Antica, Verona. This is the most elaborate of the three Scaliger monuments in Verona. As in the two earlier ones the tomb effigy is placed under a canopy surmounted by an equestrian monument. The architecture here, however, plays a far more important part than in the monument to Can Grande della Scala whose mounted figure (figure 106) dominates his tomb.

plare mortelle [handwritten]

100. **Battle scene.** From the Story of Alexander (B.M. Royal MS. 20 B xx, f. 16r.). British Museum, London. The artist's enthusiasm for gory detail, found in this scene from a French manuscript of the popular story of Alexander, can be paralleled in many contemporary descriptions in secular literature; but it must also reflect something of the brutal if colourful nature of medieval warfare.

101. **Tomb effigy of Edward III.** *c.* 1377–80. Gilt copper. Approximately life-size. Westminster abbey. If this figure of Edward III is compared with the earlier effigy of Eleanor of Castile (plate 95) it is obvious that idealisation has given way to realism. In spite of the stylisation of hair and beard an attempt at portraiture, possibly based on a death mask, has been made.

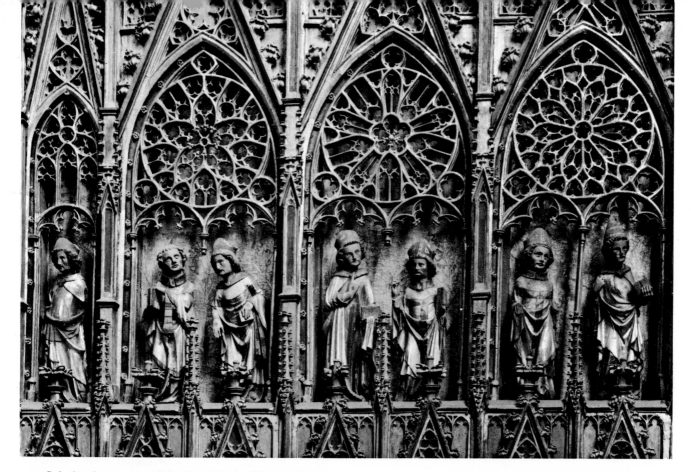

100. **Schnitzaltar.** *c.* 1330. Wood. St Maria, Oberwesel.
In this, one of the earliest surviving Schnitzaltars (carved
wooden altars), the doll-like figures are treated as separate
units set into the architectural whole—in much the same
way as the figures on a church façade (see figure 99).

were actually composed is given away by Villard de Honnecourt in his sketchbook. In what are little more than
doodles, he shows outlines drawn around abstract geometrical figures like squares, triangles and pentagons. It
is unlikely that either he or any sculptor of his time got far
beyond the stage of thinking of bodies as anything more
than outlines of this kind. The rest was simply a question of
filling in the drapery. A statue deliberately planned to be
93 seen from two views like the Strasbourg *Synagogue* was quite
exceptional. But although it suggests that an outline was
drawn on the side as well as on the front of the block, even
this stopped short of being a fully rounded statue in the
Greek sense. It is more like two high reliefs placed at right
angles to one another and then very skilfully merged together. In fact monumental Gothic statues never quite
seem to escape the residual characteristics of relief. Apart
from the method of their composition, this has something
100 to do with their being placed against walls or in niches and
tabernacles, and though we can often move slightly to left

102 (opposite). **Jean II.** *c.* 1360. 35¾ × 16 in. (91 × 41 cm.).
Louvre, Paris. This is the earliest surviving French panel
painting, and its vivid characterisation of the king—who died a
prisoner of the English—shows that as in tomb sculpture the
tendency to idealise the features of royal patrons was giving way
to an unflattering realism. The stark profile view possibly
derives from antique coins.

or right for an oblique view, there is always a point beyond
which we are not meant to go.

The first great display of monumental statues in niches
is to be seen at Wells in England (*c.* 1220–40). On the whole
the English were not impressed by French cathedral portals, to judge from the rigorous exclusion of statues from the
diminutive doorways at Wells, on the characteristically
snobbish grounds that they did not show proper respect
for the niceties of class distinction in the spiritual hierarchy.
By the 14th century, for instance at the cathedrals of Strasbourg or Bordeaux, we find the Germans and French agree-
ing with them, at least to the extent of providing proper
niches in their portals to protect the saints from profane
contagion. At Wells the niches were attached to buttresses,
and for the most part they impose a single viewpoint on the
statues. In spite of its buttresses, however, the Wells façade
is basically a screen, and by the 14th century it was recognised in Germany that the proper place for this feature was
behind the high altar. An early '*Schnitzaltar*' of this type is
at Oberwesel on the Rhine (*c.* 1330) where each figure or   *100*
pair of figures is treated like a relief set under its own canopy of Rayonnant tracery. One climax of the subsequent
development is to be found in Spanish retables around
1500. But already a century before, in Jacques de Baerze's   *102*
altar for the Duke of Burgundy at Dijon (1391), the idea
was given a new twist when the sculpture was so to speak
detached from the tracery and organised into little pictorial scenes on the Naumburg pattern. The whole altar   **72**

was in fact nothing but a sacred toy theatre. Once this new orientation was established, the way was open for the truly fantastic altarpieces of late 15th-century Germany, in which have been rightly recognised the consummation of all Gothic tendencies to concentrate the arts of architecture, sculpture and painting into a medieval *Gesamtkunstwerk*.

63 But, to return to actual figure sculpture, once the rippling undulations of the classical drapery style had been rejected at Reims, the problem was to achieve something like the same effect by other means. In spite of its casual naturalism, what makes classical drapery interesting is its subtle exploitation of balance, contrast, tension and climax, and none of this was lost on the sculptors of the next generation. They became expert at mixing patterns informally so that one sequence of folds cut across another, or the left half was the antithesis of the right half, or the top mirrored 76 the bottom. They made their figures bend and twist, so that the movement created lines of tension (without ever actually evoking the underlying anatomy). They used clasps and free hands to gather up bundles of cloth at points of special emphasis. A favourite device was to play off nests 99 of broad chevron folds against dramatic vertical shadows or cascades of frills. The place where all these possibilities were first explored was once again Reims, and this was the basis of the special reputation of that cathedral in the Gothic world. The ramifications of the various Reims styles are to be traced all over Europe, into Spain, England and Germany, as well as throughout France. Two of the most

famous variations on these themes are the *Vierge Dorée* at Amiens, and the *St Elizabeth* at Bamberg. 10

COURTLY ELEGANCE IN PARIS

Whereas it is by and large true to say that the dramatic aspects of these early and mid 13th-century statues were developed and exaggerated in Germany, in France they gradually succumbed to the cult of elegance for its own sake. To serve the French court there grew up in Paris a whole range of what must almost be called luxury arts. Apart from occasional tapestries like the set at Angers, our 94 knowledge of these is to be had chiefly from illuminated manuscripts, ivories and small statuettes in other materials, 76 the latter now almost invariably deprived of the miniature architecture in which they were originally set. The purpose of these objects was to furnish the private chapels of their aristocratic owners. Every castle, and ultimately every large house as well, had its own chapel. These now began to vie with churches in the splendour of their equipment. And with the growing influence of French fashions abroad, small-scale and therefore portable works of French art often found their way into the remoter corners of Europe. Established courts like those of England and Spain, Princes of the Church like the Archbishop of Cologne, and relative newcomers like the 14th-century despots of the northern Italian cities (in particular the Visconti of Milan) all to some extent emulated the court of France.

Though the *Virgin* on the south transept of Notre Dame in Paris was made only a few years after the one at Amiens,

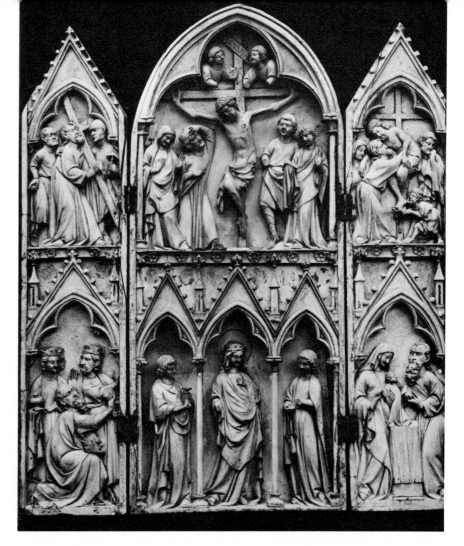

101 (opposite, left). **St Elizabeth.** *c.* 1235. Bamberg cathedral. The cascades and deep-cut folds of the draperies, with their echoes of Reims (see figure 63), provide a startling contrast to the brutal realism of the saint's face, a study in stern old age. The dramatic perception which played so large a part in German Gothic sculpture lends to this figure a power lacking in the Reims *St Elizabeth*.

102 (opposite, right). **Jacques de Baerze.** *Schnitzaltar* (detail). 1391. Wood. Dijon Museum. Instead of the isolated figures of the Oberwesel altar (figure 100), three scenes—the Adoration, the Crucifixion, and the Entombment—are here presented as though in a theatre.

103. **Triptych** from the church of S. Sulpice. Mid-14th century. Ivory. $12\frac{1}{2} \times 11\frac{1}{4}$ in. (32 × 28 cm.). Musée de Cluny, Paris. The 14th century in France saw the production of a vast number of small-scale works in ivory. Many of them, although technically of a very high quality like the one shown here, display little more than a concern with sophisticated elegance. Even the gestures of grief in the Passion scenes are formalised.

she has a better figure, is much more aristocratic, but at the same time far less of a personality. Moreover, well bred Parisian *Virgins* were evidently not expected to give way to the kinds of emotion that were permissible in remote provincial backwaters like Naumburg. Their vacuous, pretty faces are invariably untroubled by intimations of sorrow. Elegance was essentially a matter of bearing, and to the sinuous curves of Reims Paris added its own graceful backward-bending movement. This was particularly effective in statues of the *Virgin and Child*. But we may observe that the dominant effect was as much frivolity as tenderness. When we compare them with Giovanni Pisano's infinitely more serious versions of this favourite Gothic theme, we find that he went out of his way almost deliberately to destroy the impression of elegance by thrusting the heads of mother and Child towards one another, as though they were deformed by the force of the feeling that drew them together.

At its best, however, this Parisian style achieved standards of nobility that were in their way unequalled. The silver-gilt statuette of the Virgin which was made for Jeanne d'Evreux before 1339 is more than just fastidious. She may be taken to represent in their best form the courtly ideals of 14th-century society, and the fact that she is gilded reminds us that this was still an age in which precious materials and fine, gleaming finishes were appreciated as much as form. It is unlikely that Paris entirely displaced the Low Countries as the traditional headquarters of these particular skills, but so long as the French court remained

in residence there, i.e. until the crisis of the Hundred Years War, there was a constant drift of the best craftsmen in that direction. Just how much virtuosity they were called upon to lavish on the production of extravagant toys, thinly disguised as reliquaries, has now to be judged from isolated survivors like the 'Goldenes Rössel' at Altötting in Bavaria.

GOTHIC PAINTING

In its love of jewellery and bright colours, the Gothic age did not differ fundamentally from the Romanesque. Nearly all statues were painted, and so at least were selected parts of buildings. This brings us finally to the art of painting and its place in the hierarchy of the Gothic arts. To put it last once more is still perhaps no great injustice. For in Gothic eyes, as previously, the main purpose of paint was to colour surfaces, and surfaces that did not lend themselves to other forms of decoration, such as stonework and books. But even walls were covered with tapestries whenever possible, and the surest way to make a book sumptuous was to fill it with gold leaf. Any primacy which painting may have enjoyed among the arts by default of competition, up to Romanesque times, was certainly not retained by it during the Gothic centuries.

When painters painted images, they were concerned with them first and foremost as outlines, i.e. as two-dimensional shapes, and any subsequent interest in modelling or space was almost certainly subordinate—the by-product of gesture and situation. After the revival of sculpture on a large scale in the 12th century, painters no doubt found themselves called upon to provide the finishing touches to the works of their colleagues, and then, by an extension made easy through their common interest in outline drawings, to supply alternatives for statues or reliefs. It is not a simple matter to compare the relative charges made by painters and sculptors throughout the Middle Ages but, all things being equal, a picture should have been less expensive than a statue. So when we encounter a painting of something that could have been done in relief or in the round, it is likely to have been a cheap substitute—however excellent its artistic merits may seem to us. A painted wooden cross, or retable or altar-frontal 10,69 would have been made of gold and bejewelled if possible. From this point of view, painting may be said to have become a copying art, once the others were established. Even in the field of manuscript illumination, where there was an established tradition and the problems were peculiar to the trade, there is growing evidence from the 13th century onwards that the artists who were engaged in this kind of work fell more and more completely under the spell of styles and fashions which originated outside the world of books. From then on, illuminators would seem to have been professionals, closely in touch with other artists.

What provided the tremendous impetus to painting that we can observe all over Europe in the 13th century was the 84,85,86 foundation of a large number of friars' churches, and the rebuilding or refurnishing of an even larger number of other churches—not just cathedrals and abbeys, but right down to the level of parish churches. And it was for the less well endowed of these that painting was called upon to perform its more ambitious tasks. Special enterprises, like 79,95,101 the Sainte Chapelle in Paris or Westminster abbey in England, could command the resources of all the arts, and there was little inducement for painting to attempt what the others could do in more spectacular media.

Medieval painting only really started to break new ground when its own traditions were so to speak cross-fertilised with the other arts, i.e. when it tried to do what was perhaps more appropriate for sculpture and even architecture. For reasons already given, this happened 88 more extensively in Italy than elsewhere. Up to the 13th century, when Italy was in need of artistic inspiration, she was accustomed either to draw on her own considerable resources and traditions, or else to call upon the eastern Mediterranean, where Byzantium was still the artistic and cultural capital of the world. But after 1200 all this was changed. The sack of Constantinople in 1204, the growing integration of Catholic Christendom, and even to some 84,85 extent the personality and fame of St Francis of Assisi, all indirectly helped to reorientate Italy away from the Mediterranean, and toward transalpine Europe. For the first time in her history, Italy became susceptible during 98 the 13th century to artistic influences from the north. The first form which these took was of course Gothic architecture. This was already making its mark by 1220. Sculpture came much later in the century, but by the time Giovanni

Pisano produced his statues for the façade of Siena cathedral (c. 1284), it had at least one brilliant exponent. The reaction of painting to the north was, however, much more complex. For one thing the native traditions were strongly entrenched; and secondly, it was not through northern painting that the relevant influences were brought to bear on the Italians. What happened in Italy during the hundred years between 1250 and the Black Death was not the reception of a new style so much as the formation of an entirely new view as to what the art of painting was for, and 88 what it could do. These changes were so profound that, during the period in question here, the artists can scarcely have been conscious of the implications of what they were doing, which was nothing less than to repudiate the presuppositions underlying almost the whole previous history of painting in so far as it was concerned with symbolic outlines and surfaces. The outlook towards which they gradually worked their way was the theory of illusionistic 89 or representational painting: the business of the painter was in some sense to recreate visions of reality, and here 85,8 reality was not that world beyond the senses into which it had hitherto been claimed or assumed artistic imagination had the power to penetrate. It was nothing but the world of ordinary sense-perception. Subject to this immense curtailment of its scope, painting could henceforth set about the reinterpretation of its traditional Christian themes—until in the end they were no more than prodigious human events performed by heroes. No doubt to the vulgar laity this constituted an enormous improvement, like the cinema over Greek tragedy. But one can sympathise with those conservative theologians who shook their heads and regarded it all as the beginning of the end.

In committing itself to the imitation of reality, Italian painting, whether it knew it or not, was following in the footsteps of the Master of Naumburg. But there was all the 72 difference in the world between a sculptor trying to do this, and a painter—at least in the 13th century. It is therefore not surprising that the whole process took a great deal longer than one man's working lifetime. The laws of illusion proved singularly elusive. In fact during the Gothic period, only three achievements call for comment. They may be referred to as: (1) the integration of figures with the architectural or landscape backgrounds of the scenes that they enact; (2) the introduction of emotional attitudes; and (3) the construction of three-dimensional buildings, more particularly interiors. It is obvious that the first and the last of these could be, and they did in fact become, interconnected.

GIOTTO

In both Romanesque and Byzantine painting, architecture 48 and landscapes are present as the subject requires, not because all events must take place in some physical context. And when they occur, they do so as symbols rather 90 than as representations. These attitudes lingered long in Gothic painting as well. But during the 13th century,

104. **Ambrogio Lorenzetti.** *Good Government in the Country* (detail). 1337–9. Palazzo Pubblico, Siena. The subject of these frescoes decorating the old centre of civic authority in Siena is, appropriately, the effects of good and bad government in town and country. The prosperous countryside in the background of this detail is part of a panoramic view into which the foreground figures move, without any break in continuity.

84, 86

buildings and mountains begin to perform a new function. We can see this already well developed in the famous cycle of frescoes devoted to the life of St Francis in his church at Assisi, which are traditionally the work of Giotto, and were made just before 1300. In these pictures the figures are clearly regarded as being on some sort of stage, and the primary purpose of the various backgrounds is to cut off the superfluous space behind the actors. This is already very different from the golden empyrean which is the normal ambiance of Byzantine saints. But at Assisi the backgrounds do something more. They actually participate in the dramas that take place before them as marks of stress, rather like the music in a Wagnerian music-drama. Thus when St Francis repudiates his patrimony, the two groups of figures, those whom he is leaving and those whom he is about to join, are so to speak identified and accentuated by the buildings behind them, and the void in between is nothing less than the unbridgeable gulf across which St Francis cannot return. Again, in the scene where the

86

saint expels the devils from Arezzo, he and his colleagues are placed before the cathedral, while the town on the right slopes away so that its roofs continue the movement of St Francis's arm—which is in effect the direction of the miraculous power and the line of flight of the discomfited devils. Precisely the same method of composition is to be found in the documented Giottos of the Arena chapel at Padua (1304–6). Thus in the scene of the *Deposition of Christ* the hillside at the back sweeps down to converge with the mourners lamenting over the dead body. It perhaps reaches its climax in another cycle by Giotto on the

theme of St Francis, this time in the Bardi chapel in Sta **85** Croce at Florence (1320s). Here the renunciation scene is placed at the top of the wall of the chapel in a semicircular lunette. For practical reasons there is now only one building, and it is set obliquely, so that its apex fits comfortably into the curve of the frame, and its edge cleaves the stage into two separate triangular areas, in which the groups are placed. Dramatically the purpose is realised even more effectively than at Assisi.

It may seem perverse to single out this aspect of Giotto's art above all others, but it is the one that most clearly reveals his approach to picture making. The basic problem was to create a stage. The rest follows from this—the modelling that turns images into personalities, and the carefully graduated emotions that define their respective parts. To call this art Gothic, as it is now becoming fashionable to do, shows insight into the sympathies which sustained the revolutionary side of Giotto's achievement. But he was never quite Gothic in the German sense, and those for whom his gravity and grandeur used to make him the true founder of the Renaissance in Italian art were not perhaps far wrong.

The other great contemporary Italian school of painting had its headquarters at Siena. Politically, Ghibelline Siena was the inveterate enemy of Guelf Florence, and the same allegiance determined her attitude to Papal Rome. Until 1305, when the Pope withdrew to Avignon, Rome itself had been the home of another important group of painters —of whom Cavallini is the best known. Rome was the one medieval city where extensive displays of Early Christian

105. **The Annunciation.** Illuminated initial from manuscript (Clm. 6, f. 4v). Third quarter of the 14th century. Cathedral library, Prague. The cult of connoisseurship, which developed during the 14th century, led to the increasingly lavish decoration of private devotional books. Although this reached its climax in the magnificent collection of the Duke of Berry, it was not confined to France alone, as can be seen from the quality of this missal made for a Bohemian bishop.

mosaics and painting could be seen, and during the 13th century many of these were restored, replaced or emulated. This experience seems to have been the determining factor in shaping the Roman school, and to some extent its cause was taken up by Florence when the flow of patronage dried up in Rome. The artistic affiliations of Siena seem to have oscillated from one side to the other of the Rome-Florence programme. In the days after the Hohenstaufen (i.e. Ghibelline) victory at Montaperti in 1260, when one might have imagined that Siena would 'go classical', she seems in fact to have remained stubbornly loyal to what Vasari calls the '*maniera greca*', which was in effect a last link between Italy and Byzantium. On the other hand, by the first quarter of the 14th century Siena was already beginning to respond far more wholeheartedly than Florence to specific details of northern Gothic. With the establishment of a French dynasty at Naples in 1265, one would have imagined that Naples would have played a decisive part in spreading Gothic throughout Italy. But though Naples had the patronage, she does not appear to have produced artists of any considerable merit, and it was therefore Florentines like Giotto, or Sienese like Simone Martini, who figured most prominently in 14th-century Neapolitan art history. If Duccio, a slightly older con-

temporary of Giotto, is chiefly famous as an exponent of the former trend, he was nevertheless susceptible, especially in the smaller and more obviously pictorial panels of his great altarpiece, the *Maestà* for Siena cathedral (1308–11), to the varied episodes of the Gospel story. The presentation may be less dramatic than Giotto's but there is more incident, a far more vivid sense of colour and, perhaps most important of all, a sense of continuity between the foreground and the landscapes behind.

The high-water mark of Parisian Gothic influence on Italian painting is to be found in the work of another Sienese, Simone Martini. A generation younger than Duccio, he in fact ended up at the papal court at Avignon where he died in 1344. It was perhaps through Simone more than anyone else that Italian Gothic began to exercise a reciprocal influence on its French sources. This may be observed most clearly in the field of manuscript illumination. In the works of the illuminator Master Honoré who was active in Paris at the end of the 13th century and the beginning of the 14th, the figures are still set in architectural frames or against patterned backgrounds, and in spite of their modelling and the placing of one figure behind the other the effect is still very much akin to sculptured relief. A generation later, in works principally associated with the workshop of Jean Pucelle, while the figure style undergoes no drastic change, the architecture in or before which the figures are set begins to display properties that are decidedly three-dimensional, and the details of some of the buildings can only be explained in terms of Siena. During the second half of the 14th century French illuminators became progressively more interested in landscape backgrounds, and this also implies Sienese influence. The great innovator here was undoubtedly Ambrogio Lorenzetti. So far as we can tell it was Lorenzetti who took the decisive step, in his fresco of the effects of *Good Government in the Country* for the town hall at Siena (1337–9), of making a panoramic landscape the subject of the painting. Even more than in its twin devoted to *Good Government in the Town*, this picture betrays a recognition of the essential unity of foreground and background, and from this point onwards the way was open for the development of unrestricted three-dimensional illusions. Lorenzetti was also the first man to apply this outlook to the architectural interior. In his *Presentation in the Temple* (1342) we encounter the first convincing architectural vista in European painting, based on something that approximates to the perspective constructions of the 15th century.

In his capacity to evoke an impression of space on two-dimensional surfaces, Ambrogio Lorenzetti brought European painting within sight of the Renaissance. It would, however, be a mistake to speak of him as a Renaissance artist even to the same extent as Giotto, if only because (landscapes apart) his ideas on the subject of what use to make of his new space remained fundamentally Gothic. As yet no one wished to evoke new and imaginary worlds, and it was only some two generations after the

106. Can Grande della Scala.
c. 1324. Sagrato di Sta Maria Antica, Verona. Although the mounted figure above Can Grande's tomb is in the tradition of earlier equestrian monuments, its attitude of confident self-assertion is far from the concept of Imperial power symbolised in classical sculptures, or the chivalrous ideal which found expression in the Bamberg *Rider* (plate 71).

Black Death that Lorenzetti's discoveries were developed.

CONCLUSION

The sense of ambiguity that hangs over Italian painting in the 14th century was in fact symptomatic of the state of 14th-century culture as a whole. Ostensibly Europe was never more religious. But in some respects this religiosity was deceptive. In spite of the efforts of the Church to preserve the trappings of its former prestige, institutionalised Christianity was on the decline, and the more profound forms of piety were increasingly to be found at the private and personal level. The controlling factors in the cultural situation were the needs of a still dominant aristocracy and a middle class successfully aspiring to join the ranks of its social betters. For these people the inherited paraphernalia of medieval Christianity inexorably became less and less relevant. From time to time large sections of society contrived to whip themselves up into a state of religious frenzy, and artists afflicted by this excitement were always liable to produce gruesome expressionistic caricatures. But without this stimulus the old forms no longer had any real content and degenerated to the status of playthings. By comparison with what came later, this aspect of 14th-century art is apt to seem both infantile and feminine. That the people themselves were not so is becoming increasingly apparent as new historical perspectives are brought to bear on their problems, and we may therefore think of the artistic patrons of the 14th century as men in varying degrees out of sympathy with the established art forms of their time. Art was nothing more than a diversion, and for serious purposes it had little or nothing to offer. In due course they were to find the secular culture that they wanted in the idealised vision of classical antiquity which Italian humanists were already preparing for them. The fundamental difference between 14th- and 15th-century art is the absence in the former and presence in the latter of what may be called a sense of the heroic. Until men were in a position to appreciate their own achievements as something other than the prodigies of divine providence, they could have no real use for art which delighted in physical pride, strength of character or human dignity. This achievement was reserved for the Renaissance. By the end of the 14th century not only did the figure arts have at their disposal all the techniques and resources necessary for the promotion of a classical revival, but the active elements of European society were themselves ready to learn the last and most subtle of the secrets of classical antiquity—how to be in effect a new kind of man.

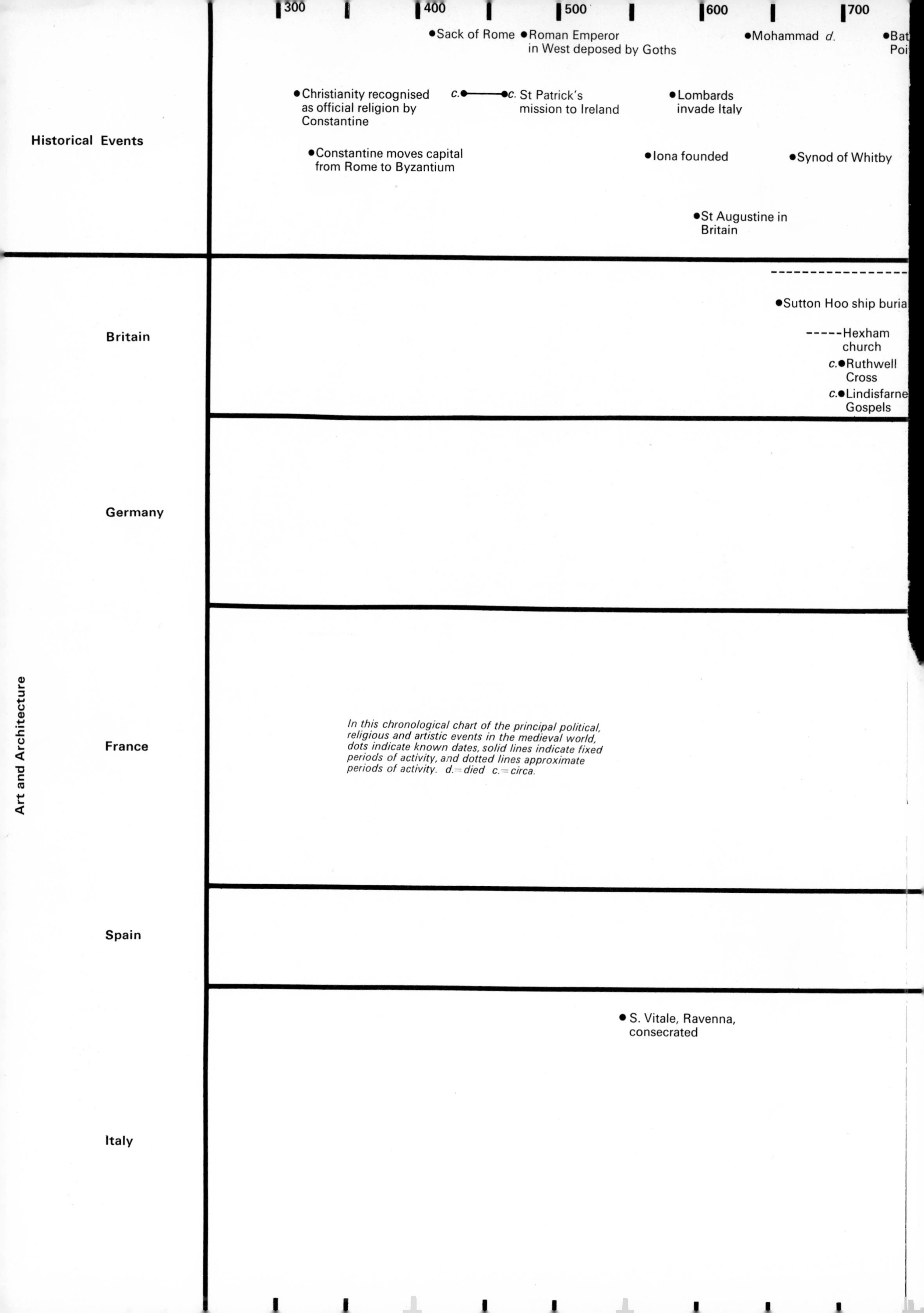

	300	**400**	**500**	**600**	**700**

Historical Events

● Sack of Rome ● Roman Emperor in West deposed by Goths ● Mohammad *d.* ● Bat Poi

● Christianity recognised as official religion by Constantine *c.*●———●*c.* St Patrick's mission to Ireland ● Lombards invade Italy

● Constantine moves capital from Rome to Byzantium ● Iona founded ● Synod of Whitby

● St Augustine in Britain

Art and Architecture

Britain

● Sutton Hoo ship burial

-----Hexham church

c.●Ruthwell Cross

c.●Lindisfarne Gospels

Germany

France

In this chronological chart of the principal political, religious and artistic events in the medieval world, dots indicate known dates, solid lines indicate fixed periods of activity, and dotted lines approximate periods of activity. d.=died c.=circa.

Spain

Italy

● S. Vitale, Ravenna, consecrated

| 800 | 900 | 1000 | 1100 | 1200 | 1300 |

●Charlemagne crowned Emperor of the West ●Treaty of St Clair sur Epte ●Battle of Hastings ●St Bernard *d.* ●St Thomas Aquinas *d.*

●Abbot Suger *d.*

...n supports Pope ...ast Lombards ●Battle of Lechfeld ●Henry IV at Canossa ●Treaty of Anagni ●Inquisition founded ●Murder of Becket ●St Francis of Assisi *d.*

●Lindisfarne sacked by Vikings ●Otto crowned Emperor ●First Crusade begins ●Third Crusade begins

●Second Crusade begins ●Albigensian Crusade begins

●Treaty of Verdun ●Fourth Lateran Council

●Magna Carta

...rence, ...d on Avon –––––––– Earls Barton church ●Winchester cathedral begun *c.*●Wells cathedral begun ●Westminster abbey rebuilding begun

––Ely cathedral begun ●Canterbury cathedral choir rebuilt ●Gloucester cathedral choir

c.●Book of Kells –––––––– Winchester Bible *after*● York minster nave rebuilt

––Gloucester candlestick ●Lincoln cathedral rebuilding begun

●———————●Durham cathedral ●———————●Salisbury cathedral

–––Palace chapel, Aachen ●St Pantaleon, Cologne, nave *c.*●Klosterneuburg abbey ●Aachen, new choir

●Godescalc Gospel *c.*●Magdeburg cathedral *c.*●Three Kings shrine (Cologne) ●St Sebaldus, Nürnberg, choir

c.●Gero Cross *c.*●St Elizabeth reliquary (Marburg)

c.●Golden Virgin of Essen (Cologne) ●Cologne cathedral begun

c.●Lothar Cross (Cologne) *c.*●Naumburg cathedral, west choir

●St Michael's, Hildesheim, bronze doors ●Strasbourg cathedral nave begun

---

––––Ebbo Gospels *c.*●Ste Foi, Conques, statuette ––––––Berzé la Ville, ––––Paris Psalter ●Albi cathedral

●Amiens cathedral begun

c.●Utrecht Psalter *c.*●Cluny, 3rd abbey *c.*●Chartres cathedral Royal Portal *c.*●St Taurin shrine, Evreux

c.●Moissac cloister ●Chartres cathedral rebuilding begun

c.●Laon cathedral begun

c.●St Savin frescoes *c.*●St Trophime, Arles, cloister ●Sainte Chapelle, Paris, finished

●Toulouse cathedral chapter house ●Le Mans cathedral begun

●Reims cathedral begun

●St Denis abbey, new choir dedicated *after*●St Gertrude shrine, Nivelles (Belgium)

●Santiago de Compostela begun ●Burgos cathedral

after●Cuenca cathedral ●León cathedral begun

●Toledo cathedral

●Duccio's *Maestà* (Siena)

–––Ferrara cathedral *c.*●Castel del Monte ●Giotto's frescoes (S. Francesco, Assisi)

●Pisa Baptistery pulpit ●A. Pisano's bronze doors (Florence Baptistery)

–––Verona cathedral ●S. Andrea, Pistoia, pulpit finished

●Siena cathedral pulpit

●Giotto's frescoes (Arena chapel, Padua)

●Sta Maria Novella, Florence, nave

●S. Martini *d.*

●G. Pisano's figures on Siena cathedral façade

●Florence cathedral begun

●Lorenzetti's *Good Government* (Siena)

Glossary

Abacus. Flat slab on top of a *capital*.

Aisle. Area flanking *nave*, *choir* or *transept* of a church, generally separated from it by an *arcade* (plate 58).

Ambulatory. Curved or polygonal *aisle*, usually enclosing the *sanctuary* of a church (plate 59, figure 55).

Apse. Semicircular or polygonal termination of a church or *chapel*, usually containing an altar (plates 27, 28).

Arcade. Row of *columns* and/or *piers* supporting a series of arches especially between the main body and *aisles* of a church (figures 40, 73).

Arch. Round-headed: Semicircular arch struck from a single centre. **Pointed:** Arch struck from two or more centres so that the arcs meet in a point at the apex. **Ogee:** *Pointed arch* with a compound curve, the lower part convex, the upper part concave, produced by striking the upper arcs from points outside the arch. Popular in the 14th and 15th centuries (plates 67, 80). **Transverse:** Arch at right angles to two walls or *arcades*, acting as a support for *vault* or roof (plates 21, 24, figure 36).

Articulation. The subdivision of a wall surface, by means of openings, and horizontal and vertical projections. See also *bay*. (Compare figures 21, 26, 61, 73.)

Ashlar. A type of masonry, using large regularly shaped blocks laid in courses.

Baptistery. Independent building, or a room or space within a church, containing a font for baptism.

Basilica. Large oblong building often with a long *nave* and *aisles*, usually with a *clearstorey*. Early Christian churches frequently took this form (plate 24).

Bay. Internal compartment of a building defined by vertical projections on the side walls or by transverse divisions of the vault or roof. A bay may include one or more arches of the *arcade* (plates 21, 24).

Boss. Ornamental knob or projection at the intersection of *vaulting ribs* (figure 78).

Buttress. Vertical mass of masonry or brickwork projecting from a wall to give support.

Flying buttress. Arch or half arch built ar right angles to a wall to transmit the lateral thrust of a *vault* or roof to an outer support (figures 59, 74).

Campanile. Italian word for a bell tower, usually free-standing.

Canopy. Roof-like cover projecting from a wall or supported on *columns*, often above figures, an altar or a sacred object (plate 16, figure 51).

Capital. Block of stone, often carved, between a *column* and an arch or superstructure.

Capital. Cushion or **Block:** *Capital* with lower part tapered to fit *column* below, leaving a semicircular face on each side. Popular in the Romanesque period (figure 31). **Corinthian:** *Capital* carved with stylised foliage (see *orders* and figure 37). **Historiated:** *Capital* carved with figures (figures 50, 51). **Moulded:** *Capital* carved with *mouldings*.

Centrally planned. Building where parts of equal length are arranged symmetrically around a central space (figure 18).

Chancel. The main body of the eastern arm of a cruciform church, or a part of the east end of a church reserved for main altar and choir (figure 78).

Chantry. An endowment made to pay for the celebration of masses for the souls of the founder or his relations. Popular in the later Middle Ages.

Chantry chapel. *Chapel* attached to or inside a church, built for the celebration of such masses, often containing the tomb of the founder.

Chapel. Either a small building used as a place of worship, or a subdivision of a church containing an altar and used for services (figure 69).

Chevet. The French word for the eastern end of a church with *apse*, *ambulatory* and usually *radiating chapels* (figure 74).

Choir. The part of the church near the main altar, usually at the east end, where divine service is sung (figure 78).

Clearstorey. The part of the *nave* wall, lit by windows, which rises above the level of the *aisle* roof (figures 73, 77).

Cloister. Square court surrounded by a covered *arcaded* passage, usually adjoining a church and linking it with monastic or collegiate domestic buildings (plate 39).

Column. Cylinder of one of more stones, or of coursed stone or brick, acting as a support, or used decoratively (figures 36, 55, 57, 58). See also *orders*.

Corbel. A block projecting from a wall to act as a support for beam or *vault*.

Corbel table. Projecting course of stone resting on a series of *corbels*.

Corinthian. See *orders* and *capital*.

Croisée d'ogives. See *ribs*.

Crossing. Space at the intersection of *nave*, east end and *transepts* often surmounted by a crossing tower, which may be a *lantern* tower (figures 30, 32).

Crypt. Chamber of a church, usually partly or completely underground, often used for burial, and sometimes as a *chapel* (plate 24, figure 31).

Decorated. The style name given to English architecture between *c.* 1270 and *c.* 1370 derived from the elaborate flowing patterns of its window *tracery* (figures 79, 80).

Dome. *Vault* based on an arch turned horizontally through 180° (figure 34).

Early English. The style name given to early Gothic architecture in England *c.* 1170–1240, characterised by *lancet* windows (plate 57, figures 44, 70).

Façade. Exterior face of the west end or *transept* end of a building often decorated with sculpture, particularly around the doorways or porches. Frequently surmounted by two or sometimes one tower (plate 38, figures 39, 41, 81, 85, 86).

Flamboyant. The name given to French Gothic architecture of the 15th century, derived from the wavy flame shape found in the *tracery* (figures 66, 81).

Gable. Triangular upper part of a wall at the end of a pitched roof.

Gallery. Upper floor, often above the *aisles* of a church, with openings into the main body of the building (plate 21, figure 61).

Hall church. Church where the *aisles* are approxi-

mately the same height as the *nave*, so the *arcade* reaches to the springing of the *vault*.

Jamb. Square sectioned support for *lintel* or arch of a door or window, often decorated. See also *orders* (medieval) (plate 38).

Lancet. Narrow pointed arched window without any subdivisions, popular in early Gothic architecture (figure 44).

Lantern. Tower or turret built without a lower vault so that its windows light the interior of the building below.

Lintel. Stone laid horizontally across an opening, often decorated (plate 38, figure 49).

Mouldings. Continuous contours forming ridges or grooves, given to projecting architectural members. The design varies according to the architectural period. See the arches in plate 61, figures 44, 73.

Narthex. Antechamber at the west end of a *nave* sometimes with an upper storey (figure 37).

Nave. Main body of a church, often flanked by *aisles*, usually lying to the west of the *crossing* and used by the lay congregation (figures 30, 57).

Niche. An ornamental recess in a wall or *screen*, usually with an arched top often containing a statue (figure 100).

Norman. The name given to Romanesque architecture in the areas ruled by the Normans, i.e. Normandy, southern Italy and Sicily from the mid-11th century, England from 1066 (plate 27, figures 26, 57).

Orders (of classical architecture). Architectural composition of *column*, *capital* and entablature (horizontal band supported by row of *columns*) whose proportions and decoration follow accepted conventions of which the best known are called Doric, Ionic and Corinthian. Elements of the classical orders (e.g. *Corinthian capitals*) were often copied in the Middle Ages (figure 37).

Orders (of a medieval door or window). Concentric series of arches receding inward to frame an opening, resting on columns or jambs (plate 38, figure 39).

Perpendicular. The name given to English late Gothic architecture (*c.* 1350–1530) derived from the vertical bars of the window *tracery* (figure 78).

Pier. Solid masonry support for an arch, of square or compound section (figures 21, 37, 73).

Pilaster. Shallow vertical right angled projection from a wall or *pier*, generally crowned by a *capital* (figure 40).

Pinnacle. Small ornamental turret crowned by a steep conical or pyramidal roof (plate 66, 68).

Radiating chapels. *Chapels* arranged radially around a curved or polygonal ambulatory (plate 57, figures 32, 33, 69).

Rayonnant. Style name given to French Gothic architecture of the mid-13th century, deriving from the window *tracery* resembling radiating spokes of a wheel (figures 72, 77).

Reliquary. Ornamental container, usually of metal, for holy relics. It may take the form of a box, a portable altar, or a *shrine* (plates 42, 65, figures 4, 75).

Reredos. Large ornamental *screen* or wall rising behind an altar.

Retable. Painted or carved panel placed behind or above an altar (plate 79, figure 102).

Ribs. Vaulting: Strengthening, or sometimes purely decorative, bands of stone projecting beneath a *vault*. See *vault* and figure 38. **Diagonal:** Intersecting ribs running along the groins of a *vault* forming a '*croisée d'ogives*'. **Transverse:** Ribs at right angles to the main direction of the vault, separating each '*croisée d'ogives*' or vault unit. **Wall:** Ribs parallel to the main direction of the vault placed between the wall and the cells of the vault.

Rood screen. Open screen at entrance to *choir* or *chancel* generally carrying a gallery, with a 'rood'—a crucifix often flanked by figures of the Virgin and St John (figure 95).

Rose window. A large circular window filled with *plate* or *bar tracery* (figures 72, 86).

Rubble. Rough unhewn masonry used for walling, or as a 'core' between wall surfaces of *ashlar*.

Sanctuary. The part of a church around the main altar at the east end.

Screen. Partition of wood or stone, often painted or carved and pierced with openings. See also *rood screen*.

Shaft. Slender *column* or *half column* attached to a wall or *pier* often acting as a subsidiary support for *vault* or roof (figure 61).

Shaft-ring. Moulded band encircling a *column* or *shaft*, sometimes linking it to another support or to a wall (plate 57, figure 61).

Shrine. Place or object of veneration, often of a commemorative nature, and often a *reliquary* (plates 65, 66, figure 75).

Spandrel. The approximately triangular space of wall on either side of an arch.

Spire. Tall pyramidal or conical structure erected on a tower (figure 85).

Splayed opening. Opening wider on one side of a wall than on the other.

Tracery. Bar: subdivision of an opening by thin bars of stone which often form intricate patterns (figures 72, 77, 80, 81). **Plate:** Groups of openings pierced in solid masonry (figure 73).

Transept. The part of a church lying at right angles to *nave* and east end, sometimes *aisled*, and usually containing *chapels* (figures 33, 69, 70).

Triforium. *Wall passage*, or a row of decorative arches, at the level between the *arcade* and *clearstorey* of a church. In early Gothic architecture sometimes found above or below a *gallery* (figures 61, 73, 77).

Trumeau. Pier supporting the centre of a *lintel*, often carved (figure 91).

Tympanum. The area of a doorway between *lintel* and arch, often carved or painted (figures 48, 60).

Vault. Arched roof of stone or brick, sometimes imitated in wood or plaster. For different types see diagrams in figure 38. See also *ribs*.

Voussoirs. Wedge-shaped stones used to construct an arch. Often decorated with carving or *mouldings* (figure 60).

Wall passage. Passage within the thickness of a wall, often found at the level of the *triforium* or *clearstorey*.

Further Reading List

General Books on Art and Architecture

Aubert, M. *La Sculpture Française au Moyen Age*, 1946 (Flammarion)

Beckwith, J. *Early Medieval Art*, 1964 (Thames and Hudson)

Bony, J., and Hürlimann, M. *French Cathedrals*, 1951 (Thames and Hudson)

Focillon, H. *Art of the West*: I, *Romanesque Art*; II, *Gothic Art*, 1963 (Phaidon)

Gall, E. *Cathedrals and Abbey Churches of the Rhine*, 1963 (Thames and Hudson)

Harvey, J. *The Cathedrals of Spain*, 1957 (Batsford)

Kidson, P., Murray, P., and Thompson, P. *A History of English Architecture*, 1965 (Penguin Books)

Pevsner, N. *An Outline of European Architecture*, 1960 (Penguin Books)

Porcher, J. *French Miniatures from Illuminated Manuscripts*, 1960 (Collins)

Rickert, M. *Painting in Britain: The Middle Ages*, 1954 (Penguin Books, Pelican History of Art)

Schramm, P. E., and Mütherich, F. *Denkmäler der Deutschen Könige und Kaiser*, 1963 (Prestel Verlag) [for plates]

Stone, L. *Sculpture in Britain: The Middle Ages*, 1955 (Penguin Books, Pelican History of Art)

Webb, G. *Architecture in Britain: The Middle Ages*, 1956 (Penguin Books, Pelican History of Art)

Carolingian, Ottonian, Anglo-Saxon and Irish Art and Architecture

Grabar, A., and Nordenfalk, C. *Early Medieval Painting*, 1957 (Skira)

Grodecki, L. *Au Seuil de l'Art Roman: L'Architecture Ottonienne*, 1958 (Colin)

Henry, F. *Irish Art in the Early Christian Period*, 1965 (Methuen)

Hinks, R. *Carolingian Art*, 1935 (Sidgwick and Jackson)

Kendrick, T. D. *Anglo-Saxon Art to AD 900*, 1938 (Methuen)

Kendrick, T. D. *Late Saxon to Viking Art*, 1949 (Methuen)

Taylor, H. M., and Taylor, J. *Anglo-Saxon Architecture*, 1965 (Cambridge U.P.)

Romanesque Art and Architecture

Boase, T. S. R. *English Art 1100–1216*, 1953 (Oxford U.P., Oxford History of English Art)

Clapham, A. W. *Romanesque Architecture in Western Europe*, 1936 (Clarendon Press)

Clapham, A. W. *English Romanesque Architecture*: I, *Before the Conquest*; II, *After the Conquest*, 1934 (Clarendon Press)

Conant, K. J. *Carolingian and Romanesque Architecture 800–1200*, 1956 (Penguin Books, Pelican History of Art)

Demus, O. *The Mosaics of Norman Sicily*, 1950 (Routledge and Kegan Paul)

Evans, J. *Cluniac Art of the Romanesque Period*, 1950 (Cambridge U.P.)

Focillon, H. *L'Art des Sculpteurs Romans*, 1964 (Presses Universitaires de France)

Grabar, A., and Nordenfalk, C. *Romanesque Painting from the 11th to the 13th Centuries*, 1958 (Skira)

Grivot, D., and Zarnecki, G. *Gislebertus, Sculptor of Autun*, 1961 (Collins/Trianon Press)

Kidson, P., and Pariser, U. *Sculpture at Chartres*, 1958 (Tiranti)

Porter, A. K. *Romanesque Sculpture of the Pilgrimage Roads*, 10 vols, 1923 (Marshall Jones)

Swarzenski, H. *Monuments of Romanesque Art*, 1955 (Chicago U.P.)

Vallery-Radot, J. *Eglises Romanes, Filiations et Echanges*, 1931 (La Renaissance du Livre)

Zarnecki, G. *English Romanesque Sculpture 1066–1140*, 1951 (Tiranti)

Zarnecki, G. *Later English Romanesque Sculpture 1140–1210*, 1953 (Tiranti)

Gothic Art and Architecture

Aubert, M. *Le Vitrail Français*, 1958 (Editions des Deux Mondes)

Branner, R. *St Louis and the Court Style*, 1965 (Zwemmer)

Brieger, P. *English Art 1216–1370*, 1957 (Oxford U.P., Oxford History of English Art)

Dupont, J., and Gnudi, C. *Gothic Painting*, 1954 (Skira)

Evans, J. *English Art 1307–1461*, 1949 (Oxford U.P., Oxford History of English Art)

Frankl, P. *Gothic Architecture*, 1962 (Penguin Books, Pelican History of Art)

Hahn, H. *Die Frühe Kirchenbaukunst der Zisterzienser*, 1957 (Mann)

Hennessy, J. Pope *Italian Gothic Sculpture*, 1955 (Phaidon)

Medieval History and Contemporary Sources and Documents

Bloch, M. *Feudal Society*, 1961 (Routledge and Kegan Paul)

Dodwell, C. R. (ed.) *Theophilus: De Diversis Artibus*, 1961 (Nelson, Nelson's Medieval Texts)

Frankl, P. *The Gothic: Literary Sources and Interpretations through Eight Centuries*, 1960 (Princeton U.P.)

Heer, F. *The Medieval World: Europe 1100–1350*, 1962 (Weidenfeld and Nicholson)

Holt, E. G. (ed.) *A Documentary History of Art*, 2 vols, 1958 (Doubleday Anchor Books)

Huizinger, J. *The Waning of the Middle Ages*, 1955 (Penguin Books)

Knowles, D. *The Evolution of Medieval Thought*, 1962 (Longmans, Green)

Southern, R. *The Making of the Middle Ages*, 1959 (Grey Arrow)

Index

Acknowledgements

The author would like to put on record his indebtedness to Mrs John Cherry and Miss Amanda Tomlinson for the enormous amount of work they put into the preparation of this book for publication; and also to Mrs Robin Benson for reading the proofs.

Photographs were provided by the following:

Colour: Nigel Atkins, London 56; Lala Aufsberg, Sonthofen im Allgau 38; Banque de Paris, Brussels 45; Bayerische Staatsbibliothek, Munich 14, 17; Bibliothèque Nationale, Paris 52; Bibliothèque Royale de Belgique, Brussels 54; British Museum, London 47, 80; Cologne Tourist Office 15, 43; Courtauld Institute of Art, London 89, 90, 100; Giraudon, Paris 9, 12, 16, 26, 29, 34, 44, 53, 65, 76, 94, 102; Paul Hamlyn Archive 35; Michael Holford, London 2, 6, 11, 22, 23, 28, 30, 31, 33, 49, 59, 61, 63, 67, 68, 70, 77, 81, 95, 96, 97; Studio Jon, Fishguard 93; A. F. Kersting, London 57, 64, 79, 91, 101; MAS, Barcelona 8, 60, 62; Hans Meile, Augsburg 32; Mondadori Press, Verona 82, 83, 87, 88, 99; Ann Munchow, Aachen 18, 66; Museo Cristiano, Brescia 4; National Gallery of Art, Washington 55; Francis Niffle, Liège 41; Picturepoint, London 92; Pierpont Morgan Library, New York 78; Photo-Wehmeyer,

Hildesheim 48; Rapho, Paris 21; Dr Hans Rathschlag, Cologne 74; Réalités, Paris 20, 27, 39; Rheinisches Landesmuseum, Bonn 3; Scala, Florence 5, 7, 10, 24, 25, 36, 58, 68, 71, 72, 73, 75, 84, 85, 86; R. Schlegelmilch, Frankfurt-am-Main 13, 42, 46; Joseph Slominsky, Essen 19; Thames and Hudson, London 1; Vasari, Rome 37, 98; John Webb, London 40, 50, 51;

Black and white: A.C.L., Brussels 14; Alinari, Florence 45, 106; Alinari-Anderson, Florence 104; Alinari-Brogi, Florence 98; Archives Photographiques, Paris 40, 49; Lala Aufsberg, Sonthofen im Allgau 91, 100; Bildarchiv Foto Marburg 2, 3, 4, 8, 18, 21, 25, 27, 34, 35, 42, 47, 53, 63, 75, 84, 90, 92, 94, 95, 102; E. Boudot-Lamotte, Paris 55, 65; British Museum, London 7, 24; Courtauld Institute of Art, London 1, 6, 10, 12, 15, 16, 20, 23, 31, 38, 43, 44, 52, 59, 60, 62, 74, 76, 79, 80, 82, 83, 96, 97, 101, 105; Giraudon, Paris 5, 19, 39, 41, 46, 48, 103; Paul Hamlyn Archive 58, 67; A. F. Kersting, London 57, 66, 73, 78; Kunsthistorische Institut, Utrecht 22; MAS, Barcelona 87; National Museum of Ireland, Dublin 11; Hugh Newbury, London 71; Normanns Kunstforlag, Oslo 9; Photo Rex, Toulouse 50; Rapho, Paris 81; Rheinisches Bildarchiv 64; Jean Roubier, Paris 26, 30, 32, 36, 37, 56, 61, 72, 85, 88, 89; Roger-Viollet, Paris 28, 51, 86; Warburg Institute, London 17; Yan, Toulouse 93, 99

Romanesque Europe in 1097

DENMARK

POLAND

Durham

ENGLAND

EAST ANGLIA

Worcester
Bury St Edmunds
Gloucester
St Albans
Winchester
Westminster
London
Canterbury

R. Rhine

Hildesheim

Paderborn
Corvey

Tournai
Liège
Aachen
Cologne
Deutz

HOLY

Stavelot

ROMAN

Forchheim

Caen
NORMANDY
Jumièges
St Clair sur Epte
Seine
Paris
Le Mans
Chartres
R. Loire
Germigny des Prés
St Benoît sur Loire

R. Meuse

R. Mosel

EMPIRE

R. Danube

Augsburg

HUNGARY

ANJOU
Tours
Auxerre
Vézelay
Fontevrault
La Charité
sur Loire
BURGUNDY
Poitiers
Autun
St Savin sur Gartempe
FRANCE
Cluny
Tournus
St Gall
Angoulême
Paray le Monial
Berzé la Ville
Macon

ALPS

S. Angelo in Formis

AQUITAINE
Clermont Ferrand
AUVERGNE
Agliate
Verona

Souillac
Aurillac
Le Puy
R. Rhône
Venice

Santiago de Compostela
Conques
Moissac
LANGUEDOC
Modena

LEÓN
NAVARRE
Toulouse
St Gilles du Gard
PROVENCE
Florence

Frómista
ARAGON
Arles

Burgos
CATALONIA

PORTUGAL
CASTILE
St Genis des Fontaines
St Martin du Canigou

PATRIMONY
OF
ST PETER
Rome

Toledo

Monte Cassino

NORMAN

ARABS

KINGDOM

MEDITERRANEAN SEA

OF

Palermo
SICILY
Monreale
Cefalù